INTRODUCING
ISSUES WITH
OPPOSING
VIEWPOINTS®

Income Inequality

M. M. Eboch, Book Editor

GREENHAVEN
PUBLISHING

Published in 2022 by Greenhaven Publishing, LLC
353 3rd Avenue, Suite 255, New York, NY 10010

Copyright © 2022 by Greenhaven Publishing, LLC

First Edition

Articles in Greenhaven Publishing anthologies are often edited for length to meet page requirements. In addition, original titles of these works are changed to clearly present the main thesis and to explicitly indicate the author's opinion. Every effort is made to ensure that Greenhaven Publishing accurately reflects the original intent of the authors. Every effort has been made to trace the owners of the copyrighted material.

Library of Congress Cataloging-in-Publication Data

Names: Eboch, M. M., editor.
Title: Income inequality / M. M. Eboch, book editor.
Description: First edition. | New York : Greenhaven Publishing, 2022. |
  Series: Introducing issues with opposing viewpoints | Includes
  bibliographical references and index. | Audience: Grades 7–12
Identifiers: LCCN 2019058540 | ISBN 9781534507197 (library binding) | ISBN
  9781534507180 (paperback)
Subjects: LCSH: Income distribution—United States—Juvenile literature.
Classification: LCC HC110.I5 I476 2022 | DDC 339.2/20973—dc23
LC record available at https://lccn.loc.gov/2019058540

Manufactured in the United States of America

Website: http://greenhavenpublishing.com

Contents

Foreword

Indulging in a wide spectrum of ideas, beliefs, and perspectives is a critical cornerstone of democracy. After all, it is often debates over differences of opinion, such as whether to legalize abortion, how to treat prisoners, or when to enact the death penalty, that shape our society and drive it forward. Such diversity of thought is frequently regarded as the hallmark of a healthy and civilized culture. As the Reverend Clifford Schutjer of the First Congregational Church in Mansfield, Ohio, declared in a 2001 sermon, "Surrounding oneself with only like-minded people, restricting what we listen to or read only to what we find agreeable is irresponsible. Refusing to entertain doubts once we make up our minds is a subtle but deadly form of arrogance." With this advice in mind, Introducing Issues with Opposing Viewpoints books aim to open readers' minds to the critically divergent views that comprise our world's most important debates.

Introducing Issues with Opposing Viewpoints simplifies for students the enormous and often overwhelming mass of material now available via print and electronic media. Collected in every volume is an array of opinions that captures the essence of a particular controversy or topic. Introducing Issues with Opposing Viewpoints books embody the spirit of nineteenth-century journalist Charles A. Dana's axiom: "Fight for your opinions, but do not believe that they contain the whole truth, or the only truth." Absorbing such contrasting opinions teaches students to analyze the strength of an argument and compare it to its opposition. From this process readers can inform and strengthen their own opinions, or be exposed to new information that will change their minds. Introducing Issues with Opposing Viewpoints is a mosaic of different voices. The authors are statesmen, pundits, academics, journalists, corporations, and ordinary people who have felt compelled to share their experiences and ideas in a public forum. Their words have been collected from newspapers, journals, books, speeches, interviews, and the Internet, the fastest growing body of opinionated material in the world.

Introducing Issues with Opposing Viewpoints shares many of the well-known features of its critically acclaimed parent series, Opposing

Viewpoints. The articles allow readers to absorb and compare divergent perspectives. Active reading questions preface each viewpoint, requiring the student to approach the material thoughtfully and carefully. Photographs, charts, and graphs supplement each article. A thorough introduction provides readers with crucial background on an issue. An annotated bibliography points the reader toward articles, books, and websites that contain additional information on the topic. An appendix of organizations to contact contains a wide variety of charities, nonprofit organizations, political groups, and private enterprises that each hold a position on the issue at hand. Finally, a comprehensive index allows readers to locate content quickly and efficiently.

Introducing Issues with Opposing Viewpoints is also significantly different from Opposing Viewpoints. As the series title implies, its presentation will help introduce students to the concept of opposing viewpoints and learn to use this material to aid in critical writing and debate. The series' four-color, accessible format makes the books attractive and inviting to readers of all levels. In addition, each viewpoint has been carefully edited to maximize a reader's understanding of the content. Short but thorough viewpoints capture the essence of an argument. A substantial, thought-provoking essay question placed at the end of each viewpoint asks the student to further investigate the issues raised in the viewpoint, compare and contrast two authors' arguments, or consider how one might go about forming an opinion on the topic at hand. Each viewpoint contains sidebars that include at-a-glance information and handy statistics. A Facts About section located in the back of the book further supplies students with relevant facts and figures.

Following in the tradition of the Opposing Viewpoints series, Greenhaven Publishing continues to provide readers with invaluable exposure to the controversial issues that shape our world. As John Stuart Mill once wrote: "The only way in which a human being can make some approach to knowing the whole of a subject is by hearing what can be said about it by persons of every variety of opinion and studying all modes in which it can be looked at by every character of mind. No wise man ever acquired his wisdom in any mode but this." It is to this principle that Introducing Issues with Opposing Viewpoints books are dedicated.

Introduction

"Most of these low-wage workers receive no health insurance, sick days, or pension plans from their employers. They can't get ill and have no hope of retiring."

—Kimberly Amadeo, President of World Money Watch.

Americans like to believe in equality. We live in a country where anyone can get rich, where anyone can become president, where everyone can imagine the future they want and work to achieve it. The American dream promises that we all have the opportunity for prosperity and success. It doesn't matter where you were born, or what class you were born into. You can achieve success through hard work, sacrifice and taking risks—not by random chance or belonging to the right social group.

Does America truly offer equal opportunity for everyone?

The statistics don't support this promise.

Income inequality is a difference in income between the rich and the poor. America's top 10 percent of earners now bring in more than nine times as much income as the bottom 90 percent. The top 0.1% of earners take in 188 times as much as the bottom 90 percent. In large companies such as Walmart and McDonald's, top officers receive at least one thousand times the pay of the average workers. This pay gap has been growing in recent decades.

An even greater gap exists between the top 10 percent and bottom 10 percent of Americans when it comes to wealth. Wealth includes the value of homes, stocks, and other possessions not included in statistics about income. People who have extra money can invest in ways that make more money, such as buying stocks and bonds, or buying property as an investment. People without extra money to invest lose this way of making more money. This tends to keep wealth in families that are already wealthy.

Meanwhile, poor people tend to stay poor. In the United States, an estimated 140 million people (43.5 percent of the total population) are either poor or low-income. Over 38 million live in poverty.

People in poverty often have worse health and live shorter lives. Some people assume that those living in poverty deserve their place, because they refuse to work hard, or at all. However, many factors play into poverty. Numbers vary by year and how they are calculated, but it can be estimated that over 40 percent of people in poverty hold jobs. About 19 percent do not work due to a disability, over 30 percent are children, and 6.5 percent are retired. Only a small percentage are unemployed. Someone can work full-time at the federal minimum wage and fall below the poverty level if they are supporting children. Many people struggle to make ends meet while working full time, simply because they do not earn enough money at their jobs.

Families living in poor communities tend to stay poor, because young people don't have access to good educations or social services. Children with disabilities such as dyslexia or hearing problems may not get diagnosed and treated in a timely manner. Teenagers don't have the same networking opportunities that could lead to internships or jobs. If poverty keeps young people out of college, they will likely never earn as much as college graduates. Americans with college degrees earn 84 percent more than those with only high school degrees. These factors tend to mean that most children born in poverty will stay there.

Poor communities are largely made up of people of color. This is one reason race has a dramatic effect on income. If young people of color manage to get out of their poor community, attend college, and enter the professional workforce, they may still face discrimination. Technically, laws prohibit discrimination based on race, color, national origin, religion, and sex. In reality, the laws don't cover every company and aren't always enforced. Studies have shown that racial bias still plays an effect in hiring practices, promotions, and raises. White and Asian workers make over 30 percent more than black and Latino workers, on average. That number can be higher or lower depending on how segregated a city is. Laws alone have not been enough to erase centuries of racism.

Income is also affected by gender. Women make up almost half of the country's workforce. They comprise 63 percent of the workers who earn the federal minimum wage, but only 27 percent of the top 10 percent of earners. Research suggests that women still earn only

$.82 or less for every dollar men make, even when they do exactly the same work. This gender pay gap is caused by pay discrimination, a bias against working mothers, and occupational segregation, where women are kept out of higher-paying industries. According to the American Association of University Women (AAUW), "Employer practices—such as using prior salary history in setting current pay and prohibiting employees from discussing their wages—compound the problem." Women also tend to hold more college debt and have less retirement savings.

The pay gap is even higher for most women of color. Black women are paid about 62 percent of what white men make. American Indian and Alaska native women make 57 percent, while Hispanic women make just 54 percent of what a white man makes.

Many factors contribute to the controversial issue of income inequality. The government, businesses, experts, and ordinary workers can hold a wide variety of opinions. Is income inequality a serious problem, or part of the natural economic order? Should we focus more on reducing the extreme incomes of the top one percent, or on raising the minimum wage? Is it even possible to close the pay gap between the rich and poor? If so, how?

Experts suggest a variety of responses, from higher taxes on the rich to ending segregation to investing in education or providing more credit. Exploring the issues through research, philosophical discussions, and personal experience can help individuals determine their answer. The current debates are explored in *Introducing Issues with Opposing Viewpoints: Income Inequality*, shedding light on this ongoing contemporary issue.

Chapter 1

Why Do We Have Income Inequality?

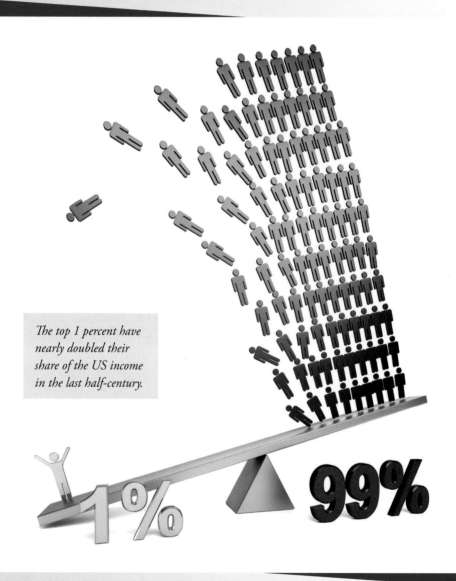

The top 1 percent have nearly doubled their share of the US income in the last half-century.

Viewpoint

1

Income Inequality Shows the Unfairness in American Jobs

"America's top 10 percent now average more than nine times as much income as the bottom 90 percent."

Inequality.org

In the following viewpoint, Inequality.org provides an overview of income inequality. The authors explain the difference between income and wealth. The viewpoint compares the income of the average American to that of the richest. It notes some of the factors that have contributed to growing income inequality. These include tax breaks that favor the rich and the weakening of unions. A trade union or labor union is an association of workers, typically in a particular field of work. The union bargains with employers on salaries, benefits, and other factors. Inequality.org tracks inequality-related news and views. It is sponsored by the Institute for Policy Studies, a progressive think tank.

AS YOU READ, CONSIDER THE FOLLOWING QUESTIONS:
1. What is income, and how does it differ from wealth?
2. How do the richest Americans compare to the majority in terms of income?
3. Who benefited most from 2017 tax cuts? Why?

I n the United States, the income gap between the rich and everyone else has been growing markedly, by every major statistical measure, for more than 30 years.

Income Inequality

Income includes the revenue streams from wages, salaries, interest on a savings account, dividends from shares of stock, rent, and profits from selling something for more than you paid for it. Unlike wealth statistics, income figures do not include the value of homes, stock, or other possessions. Income inequality refers to the extent to which income is distributed in an uneven manner among a population.

Income disparities have become so pronounced that America's top 10 percent now average more than nine times as much income as the bottom 90 percent. Americans in the top 1 percent tower stunningly higher. They average over 39 times more income than the bottom 90 percent. But that gap pales in comparison to the divide between the nation's top 0.1 percent and everyone else. Americans at this lofty level are taking in over 188 times the income of the bottom 90 percent.

Over the past five decades, the top 1 percent of American earners have nearly doubled their share of national income. Meanwhile, the official poverty rate for all U.S. families has merely inched up and down. The official poverty rate understates the number of people in the world's richest country who have trouble making ends meet. An estimated 43.5 percent of the total U.S. population (140 million people) are either poor or low-income.

The nation's highest 0.01 percent and 0.1 percent of income-earners have seen their incomes rise much faster than the rest of the top 1 percent in recent decades. Both of these ultra-rich groups saw their

US Average Income, 2017. Top 0.1% Takes in 188 Times as Much Income as Bottom 90%

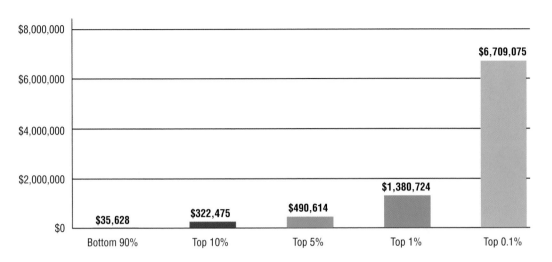

Source: Emmanuel Saez, UC Berkeley

incomes drop immediately after the financial crashes of 1929 and 2008, but they had a much swifter recovery after the more recent crisis. Income concentration today is as extreme as it was during the "Roaring Twenties."

The Congressional Budget Office defines before-tax income as "market income plus government transfers," or, quite simply, how much income a person makes counting government social assistance. Analysts have a number of ways to define income. But they all tell the same story: The top 1 percent of U.S. earners take home a disproportionate amount of income compared to even the nation's highest fifth of earners.

Since 1979, the before-tax incomes of the top 1 percent of America's households have increased more than seven times faster than bottom 20 percent incomes.

The Congressional Budget Office defines after-tax income as "before-tax income minus federal taxes." After taxes, top 1 percent incomes were already increasing faster than for other Americans. This gap will likely grow even wider as a result of the 2017 Republican tax

In the mid-20th-century United States, the middle class thrived.

cuts, which disproportionately benefit the wealthy. According to the Institute on Taxation and Economic Policy, the richest 1 percent of Americans are expected to receive 27 percent of the benefits of the tax cuts in 2019.

The higher the U.S. income group, the larger the share of that income is derived from investment profits. By contrast, Americans who are not among the ultra-rich get the vast majority of their income from wages and salaries. This disparity has contributed significantly to increasing inequality because of the preferential tax treatment of long-term capital gains. Currently, the top marginal tax rate for the richest Americans is 37 percent, while the top rate for long-term capital gains is just 20 percent.

Wage Inequality

Between 1979 and 2007, paycheck income for those in the richest 1 percent and 0.1 percent exploded. The wage and salary income for these elite groups dipped after the 2008 financial crisis but have nearly regained their pre-crisis value. Meanwhile, the bottom 90 percent of earners have seen little change in their average income, with just a 22 percent increase from 1979 to 2017.

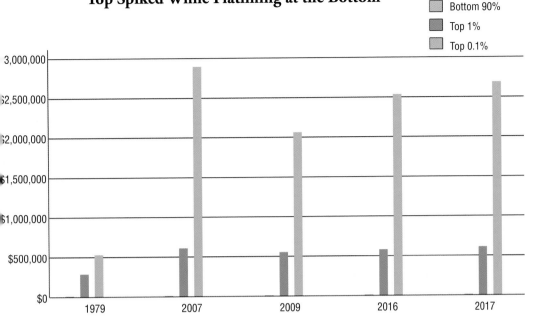

Average Annual Wages, 2017. Paychecks at the Top Spiked While Flatlining at the Bottom

Legend:
- Bottom 90%
- Top 1%
- Top 0.1%

Source: Economic Policy Institute

Productivity has increased at a relatively consistent rate since 1948. But the wages of American workers have not, since the 1970s, kept up with this rising productivity. Worker hourly compensation has flat-lined since the mid-1970s, increasing just 23 percent from 1979 to 2017, while worker productivity has increased 138 percent over the same time period.

One factor in the widening income divide is the decline of U.S. labor unions. As the share of the workforce represented by a union has declined to less than 11 percent since their peak in the 1940s and 1950s, those at the top of the income scale have increased their power to rig economic rules in their favor, further increasing income inequality.

Men make up an overwhelming majority of top earners across the U.S. economy, even though women now represent almost half of the country's workforce. Women comprise just 27 percent of the top 10 percent, and their share of higher income groups runs even smaller. Among the top 1 percent, women make up slightly less than 17 percent of workers, while at the top 0.1 percent level, they make up only 11 percent.

Racial discrimination in many forms, including in education, hiring, and pay practices, contributes to persistent earnings gaps. As of the last quarter of 2018, the median White and Asian worker made more than 30 percent as much as the typical Black and Latino worker.

Wall Street banks doled out $31.4 billion in bonuses to their 176,900 New York-based employees in 2017, which amounts to more than two and a half times the combined earnings of all 884,000 Americans who work full-time at the current federal minimum wage of $7.25 per hour. The Wall Street bonuses come on top of salaries, which averaged $422,500 in 2017. Shifting resources into the pockets of low-wage workers would give the economy a bigger bang for the buck than increases in Wall Street bonuses. To meet basic needs, low-wage workers have to spend nearly every dollar they earn, creating beneficial economic ripple effects. The wealthy, by contrast, can afford to squirrel away more of their earnings.

CEO-Worker Pay Gaps

CEO pay has been a key driver of rising U.S. income inequality. Corporate executives head about two-thirds of America's richest 1 percent of households.

With U.S. unions playing a smaller economic role, the gap between worker and CEO pay has exploded since the 1970s. In 2017, the CEO-worker pay gap was nearly nine times larger than in 1980. According to the AFL-CIO, S&P 500 firm CEOs were paid 361 times as much as average U.S. workers in 2017. CEO pay averaged $13.94 million, compared to average worker pay of $38,613. In 1980, the average big company CEO earned just 42 times as much as the average U.S. worker.

In 2018, publicly held U.S. corporations were required to report the ratio between their CEO's compensation and the firm's median worker pay. Thirty-three firms reported pay gaps larger than 1,000 to 1, including Walmart, McDonald's, and many other highly profitable corporations.

The CEO pay explosion contrasts sharply with trends at the bottom end of the U.S. wage scale. Congress has not passed a raise in the minimum wage for more than a decade. The federal minimum wage for restaurant servers and other tipped workers has been frozen at just $2.13 per hour since 1991. Twenty-four states have raised their tipped minimum, while retaining this two-tier system, and eight states have eliminated the subminimum tipped wage altogether. But in 18 states, the tipped minimum is still $2.13. While employers are technically supposed to make up the difference if workers don't earn enough in tips to reach the $7.25 federal minimum, this rule is largely unenforced.

EVALUATING THE AUTHOR'S ARGUMENTS:

This viewpoint compares the income of average Americans to the income of the richest Americans. What point are the authors trying to make? How does the inclusion of many statistics help make that point? Do you think the use of statistics is more or less powerful than sharing personal stories? Why?

The Rich Get Richer and the Poor Stay Poor

Jeff Spross

"So the best way to enrich yourself is to already be wealthy."

In the following viewpoint, Jeff Spross argues that an even greater gap exists between the top 10 percent and the bottom 10 percent of Americans when it comes to wealth. This is partly due to capital gains—profits from the sale of an asset, such as property, or an investment, such as stocks or bonds. People who have money can invest that money in ways that make more money. People without money to invest lose this way of making more money. This tends to keep wealth in families that are already wealthy. The author ends with some radical suggestions for redistributing wealth. Jeff Spross is the economics and business correspondent at TheWeek.com, a weekly news magazine.

AS YOU READ, CONSIDER THE FOLLOWING QUESTIONS:
1. How has the wealth of the bottom 10 percent of Americans changed in recent decades?
2. In what ways does wealth transfer from one generation to the next in the same family?
3. How severe is the racial wealth gap? Why?

"Wealth inequality is even worse than income inequality," by Jeff Spross, The Week Publications Inc, August 10, 2017. Reprinted by permission.

Income can pay the bills, but it only goes so far. Wealth, which is often passed down from generation to generation, has greater impact.

You probably know the numbers on income inequality by now: The share of all income going to the top 1 percent of Americans now stands at around 20 percent, which is a big and disturbing number.

But what about *wealth* inequality?

Income is a relatively straightforward matter of wages and compensation. Wealth is more mercurial: It can be a physical asset like a car, house, or land. But it can also be a stock or bond or other financial asset.

The effects of wealth also go much deeper: If you own a piece of land, you can decide what uses that land gets put to. Same thing if you own a building. If you own someone else's debt, you have tremendous legal power over their livelihood. If you own shares in a company, you have input into its governance: Where does it invest? Who does it hire? What does it pay? Income decides your standard of living, but wealth gives you control over the shape and future course of the economy.

And if you think income inequality is bad, well, you ain't seen nothing yet.

As of 2015, the top 1 percent of American households in terms of wealth ownership enjoy 35 percent of the pie all by themselves. The top 10 percent own a staggering *76 percent* of all wealth.

Furthermore, from 1963 to 2013, families in the bottom 10 percent of wealth ownership went from having no wealth at all on average to being $2,000 in debt. Over the same time period, the average wealth of the top 10 percent grew four times over. For the top 1 percent, it grew six times over. These shifts are far larger than the changes in the distribution of income over the same time frame.

But these two inequalities also feed into one another. Capital gains and other returns are a form of income, for example, and they've arguably been the biggest driver of rising income inequality since at least the 1990s. On the flip side, the more income you have, the more wealth-generating assets you can buy, leading to even more income. The top 1 percent's share of all income generated from wealth holdings has been rising for decades. And by 2014, 58.9 percent of all income going to the top 1 percent was income from wealth.

The equivalent number for the bottom *half* of all Americans was just 5.1 percent.

So the best way to enrich yourself is to *already be wealthy*. Which is kind of perverse, since income from wealth is income you don't have to lift a finger to earn. (You have to wonder if this bothers all the commentators and politicians who regularly worry that government aid to poor people discourages work.)

As a result of all this, wealth has a tendency to just transfer endlessly from one generation to the next in the same family. A big part is obviously outright inheritance. But there are subtler ways as well: "Wealthier families are better positioned to afford elite education, access capital to start a business, finance expensive medical procedures, reside in higher-amenity neighborhoods, exert political influence through campaign contributions, purchase better legal representation, leave a bequest, and withstand financial hardship resulting from an emergency," wrote Darrick Hamilton, an economist at the New School. All of which vastly improves the chances that the next generation can build up a wealth stock of their own.

So, not surprisingly, socioeconomic mobility in America is incredibly sclerotic. If you're born into the bottom fifth of the income ladder, the chances you'll stay there are 43 percent. Your chances of breaking into the top fifth are 4 percent. For people born into the top fifth, the numbers are effectively reversed. "In a capitalist system, if you lack capital, it just locks in inequality," Hamilton said.

Then there's the racial wealth gap: As of 2013, the median white household had $141,900 in wealth, while the median black household had a

paltry $11,000. The median Hispanic household had $13,700. And the gaps have actually increased since the mid-2000s, mostly because household wealth for blacks and Hispanics nosedived. These disparities are much larger than the racial gap in income, and their consequences are profound. It is arguably the clearest and most concise evidence we have that the historic damage done to black Americans by slavery, segregation, and Jim Crow is far from repaired.

So what's there to be done about wealth inequality?

Well, first off, education or "skills" or whatever won't help. If we equalized education levels between black and white Americans, we'd barely dent the racial wealth gap. Rather, wealth inequality is about how our society distributes the power and property rights that ultimately make up wealth ownership, and how easily that ownership perpetuates across generations.

That's also the challenge, because this implicates huge swaths of society. You could try a number of different, interlocking policies: Massively hike the highest tax rates on income from capital gains and labor. Strengthen the inheritance tax or just tax wealth specifically. Close tax giveaways like the mortgage interest deduction, which spend hundreds of billions every year helping already-wealthy households build up even more wealth. Reform copyright and patent laws, which let powerful companies extract endless money out of everything from software ideas to media images. Or create some sort of public option for banking, to help the tens of millions of Americans who have little-to-no access to basic banking services. I could go on.

But Hamilton himself is pushing a particularly elegant idea: "baby bonds." Every American would be given a savings account at birth, directly funded out of the U.S. Treasury Department. How much money the account is stocked with would be scaled up or down depending on the wealth circumstances the child is born into—with the least wealthy children receiving as much as $50,000 or $60,000. Once the child is a legal adult, they can spend the money on certain "clearly defined asset enhancing activities," such as getting an education, buying a house, starting a business, etc. Think of baby bonds as the third piece of a triumvirate of "big idea" reforms that would reshape the economy, alongside a universal basic income and a federal job guarantee.

The point here is this: As important as income is, who owns wealth ultimately determines who *rules*. And that kind of inequality is arguably the most destructive inequality of all.

EVALUATING THE AUTHOR'S ARGUMENTS:

In this viewpoint, author Jeff Spross suggests some major changes to government policy in order to redistribute wealth. Does the author convince you that redistributing wealth is important or valuable? If so, how would you go about it, if you had the choice? If not, why not?

The Global Economy Affects the United States

"Many of the causes of U.S. income inequality can be traced to an underlying shift in the global economy."

Kimberly Amadeo

In the following viewpoint, Kimberly Amadeo notes that many people do not make enough money to pay for their basic needs, such as health care. She mentions several causes or possible causes for rising income inequality in the United States. Some government policies have helped businesses more than workers. The global economy also affects the US economy. Many companies have outsourced jobs to other countries, where labor is cheaper. As other countries develop, their wealth rises. This takes wealth away from the US, argues the author, and the poorest people suffer the most. Kimberly Amadeo is the president of World Money Watch and an expert in economic analysis.

AS YOU READ, CONSIDER THE FOLLOWING QUESTIONS:
1. How does health care inequality increase the cost of medical care for everyone?
2. How has cheap labor in other countries affected US workers?
3. How does education affect a person's earning potential?

"Income Inequality in America: Causes of Income Inequality," by Kimberly Amadeo, Dotdash Publishing Family, June 25, 2019. Reprinted by permission.

The top 10 percent averaged more than nine times as much income as the bottom 90 percent. One-quarter of American workers make less than $10 per hour. That creates an income below the federal poverty level. These are the people who wait on you every day. They include cashiers, fast food workers, and nurse's aides. Or maybe they *are* you.

The rich got richer through the recovery from the 2008 financial crisis. In 2012, the top 10 percent of earners took home 50 percent of all income. That's the highest percentage in the last 100 years. The top 1 percent took home 20 percent of the income, according to a study by economists Emmanuel Saez and Thomas Piketty.

By 2015, America's top 10 percent already averaged more than nine times as much income as the bottom 90 percent. And Americans in the top 1 percent averaged over 40 times more income than the bottom 90 percent. The chart below shows a breakdown of average household incomes ranging from the bottom 90 percent to the top .1 percent.

While the average family income grew 25.7 percent from 1993 to 2015, 52 percent of that total growth was accrued by the top 1 percent of the population. The chart below tracks average income growths and losses during the 22-year period, and then calculates how much of that total growth was accrued by the top 1 percent of the population.

Income Inequality Facts

From 2000 through 2006, the number of Americans living in poverty increased 15 percent. By 2006, almost 33 million workers earned less than $10 per hour. Their annual income is less than $20,614. This is below the poverty level for a family of four.

Most of these low-wage workers receive no health insurance, sick days, or pension plans from their employers. They can't get ill and have no hope of retiring. The resultant health care inequality increases the cost of medical care for everyone. People who can't afford preventive care wind up in the hospital emergency room. In 2009, half of the people (46.3 percent) who used a hospital said they went because they had no other place to go. They use the emergency room as their primary care physician. The hospitals passed this cost along to Medicaid.

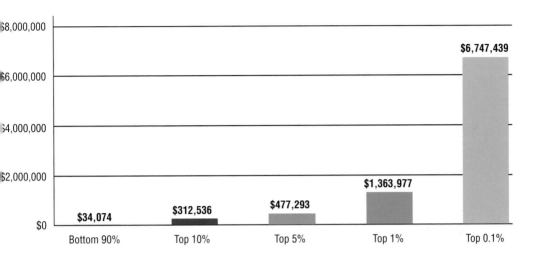

Average US Household Income, 2015

Source: Inequality.org

Americans in the top 1 percent averaged over 40 times more income than those in the bottom 90 percent.

During this same period, average wages remained flat. That's despite an increase of worker productivity of 15 percent. Corporate profits increased 13 percent per year, according to "The Big Squeeze" by Steven Greenhouse.

Between 1979 and 2007, household income increased 275 percent for the wealthiest 1 percent of households. It rose 65 percent for the top fifth. The bottom fifth only increased 18 percent. That's true even after "wealth redistribution" which entails subtracting all taxes and adding all income from Social Security, welfare, and other payments.

Since the rich got richer faster, their piece of the pie grew larger. The wealthiest 1 percent increased their share of total income by 10 percent. Everyone else saw their piece of the pie shrink by 1-2 percent. Even though the income going to the poor improved, they fell further behind when compared to the richest. As a result, economic mobility is worsening.

Real Income Growth by Group, 1993-2015
Fraction Total Growth (or Loss) Top 1%

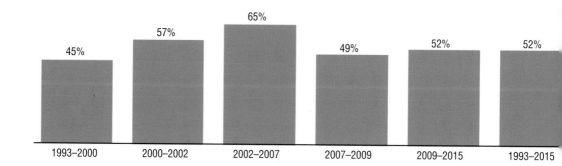

Emmanuel Saez, UC Berkeley

The fraction of total growth column shows what percentage of the average income real growth was gained or lost by the top 1 percent. From 1993 to 2015, average real family income grew by 25.7 percent. Of that growth, 52 percent was accrued by the top 1 percent, and 48 percent was accrued by the bottom 99 percent.

The biggest discrepancy was Marathon Petroleum. Its CEO made $19.7 million, 935 times that of the median worker's pay of $21,034. Whirlpool's CEO made $7.1 million, 356 times that of its average employee pay of $19,906. Honeywell's average worker pay is $50,000. Its CEO made $16.8 million, or 333 times that.

What Is to Blame

Income inequality is blamed on cheap labor in China, unfair exchange rates, and jobs outsourcing. Corporations are often blamed for putting profits ahead of workers. But they must to remain competitive. U.S. companies must compete with lower-priced Chinese and Indian companies who pay their workers much less. As a result, many companies have outsourced their high-tech and manufacturing jobs overseas. The United States has lost 20 percent of its factory jobs since

2000. These were traditionally high-er-paying union jobs. Service jobs have increased, but these are much lower paid.

Education is also a powerful factor in improving economic mobility. Education increases the income that generates greater economic growth. Over a lifetime, Americans

with college degrees earn 84% more than those with only high school degrees. A McKinsey study found that this achievement gap has cost the U.S. economy more than all recessions since the 1970s.

Deregulation means less stringent investigations into labor disputes. That also benefits businesses more than wage earners.

During the 1990s, companies went public to gain more funds to invest in growth. Managers must now produce ever-larger profits to please stockholders. For most companies, payroll is the largest budget line item. Reengineering has led to doing more with fewer full-time employees. It also means hiring more contract and temporary employees. Immigrants, many in the country illegally, fill more low-paid service positions. They have less bargaining power to demand higher wages.

President Trump's tax plan has helped businesses and investors more than wage earners. This creates structural inequality.

Wal-Mart is the nation's largest employer at 1.4 million. Unfortunately, it has set new standards for reducing employee pay and benefits. Its competitors must follow suit to provide the same "Low Prices."

In recent years, the Federal Reserve deserves some of the blame. Record-low interest rates were supposed to spur the housing market, making homes more affordable. While that is the case, housing prices have leveled off in recent years. The average American still doesn't have enough income to buy a home. This is especially true for younger people who typically form new households. Without good jobs, they're stuck living at home or with roommates.

By keeping Treasury rates low, the Fed created an asset bubble in stocks. This helped the top 10 percent, who own 91 percent of the wealth in stocks and bonds. Other investors have been buying commodities, driving food prices up 40 percent since 2009. This hurts the bottom 90 percent, who spend a greater percentage of their income on food.

Take a Global Perspective

Many of the causes of U.S. income inequality can be traced to an underlying shift in the global economy. Emerging markets incomes are increasing. Countries such as China, Brazil, and India are becoming more competitive in the global marketplace. Their work-forces are becoming more skilled. Also, their leaders are becoming more sophisticated in managing their economies. As a result, wealth is shifting to them from the United States and other developed countries.

This shift is about lessening global income inequality. The richest 1 percent of the world's population has 40 percent of its wealth. Americans hold 25 percent of that wealth. But China has 22 percent of the world's population and 8.8 percent of its wealth. India has 15 percent of its population and 4 percent of its wealth.

As other countries become more developed, their wealth rises. They are taking it away from the United States, the European Union, and Japan. In America, the least wealthy bear the brunt.

Solutions

Trying to prevent U.S. companies from outsourcing will not work. It is punishing them for responding to global redistribution of wealth. Neither will protectionist trade policies or walls to prevent immigrants from entering illegally.

The United States must accept that global wealth redistribution is occurring. Those in the top fifth of the U.S. income bracket must realize that those in the bottom two-fifths cannot bear the brunt forever.

The government should provide the bottom two-fifths access to education and employment training. Investing in human capital is the best way to increase individual wealth and improve the labor force. Equity in education would bring everyone up to at least a minimum

standard. It would be a better solution than increasing welfare benefits or providing a universal basic income.

Congress can raise taxes on the top fifth to pay for it. It should
make these changes now so that the transition is gradual and healthy
for the economy overall.

**EVALUATING THE AUTHOR'S
ARGUMENTS:**

In this viewpoint, author Kimberly Amadeo explores how
the global economy affects poverty in the United States.
How does she think the US government should address
this? Do you agree with her conclusions? Why or why not?

Race and Economic Inequality Are Intertwined

"The family income gap between blacks and whites today remains at almost exactly the level it was in the 1960s."

Robert Manduca

In the following viewpoint, Robert Manduca explores how race affects economic equality. Racial gaps have closed in many areas, such as high school test scores and college attainment. Yet an income gap continues between blacks and whites, due to both discrimination and the overall increase in income inequality. Many African Americans have entered the middle class; however that does not have the rewards it did earlier in US history. Only a tiny percent of the population has grown much richer. Robert Manduca is a PhD student in sociology and social policy at Harvard University.

AS YOU READ, CONSIDER THE FOLLOWING QUESTIONS:

1. What factors contribute to economic inequality for African Americans in particular?
2. How has the weakening of the middle class negatively affected African Americans?
3. If income inequality hadn't increased, how would African American family income compare to white family income today?

Fifty years after the U.S. civil rights movement, racial economic inequality remains an undeniable force in American life. The family income gap between blacks and whites today remains at almost exactly the level it was in the 1960s—just one of many indicators of the remarkably little progress toward racial convergence in family income. Many well-documented factors contribute to this income gap, among them ongoing discrimination in the labor market, racial differences in family structure, and segregation by occupation and neighborhood.

One underappreciated factor that contributes to the racial income gap is the lack of equitable growth in the U.S. economy at large. Since the 1970s, the share of national income going to the richest 1 percent almost doubled, while wages for most Americans remained stagnant. As I show in a recent paper, "Income Inequality and the Persistence of Racial Economic Disparities," rising income inequality has disproportionately harmed African Americans, negating substantial improvements in relative terms and preventing what would otherwise have been a meaningful, if incomplete, convergence in incomes between blacks and whites. In short, inequitable growth over the past few decades is a major driver of our nation's persistent racial income gap.

Let's first look at the average income for African Americans as a fraction of the average income for whites over time. Whether we choose mean or median, family or household income, the picture is the same: There has been virtually no improvement in the average ratio of black to white income over time. Focusing on median family income, in 1968, just after the civil rights movement, the median African American family income was 57 percent of the median white American family income. In 2016, the ratio was 56 percent. The utter lack of progress is striking.

It's also a bit puzzling because racial gaps in many other social outcomes have contracted since the 1960s: College attainment, high school test scores, and life expectancy all have seen some convergence between blacks and whites, though progress in these areas is by no means complete.

So, why has there been so little progress toward equalizing incomes? Well, it turns out that the intransigent racial income gap

Despite progress in employment opportunities and income levels, African Americans continue to be burdened by a racial income gap.

is the result of two opposing trends. On the one hand, blacks have made real progress climbing to higher positions on the income distribution. From 1968 to 2016, the median African American climbed from the 25th percentile of the national family income distribution to the 35th percentile. While this progress is nowhere near complete, it was enough to narrow the gap in income ranks between blacks and whites by almost a third. In the 1960s, the large majority of whites earned more than the typical black person. By 2016, that proportion had declined substantially. This progress came despite continued racial disparities in parental wealth, access to educational resources, and treatment in the labor market.

On the other hand, just as African Americans were entering the ranks of the middle class in large numbers for the first time, broader economic forces were undermining the financial security of families across all races.

FAST FACT

The median family income for African Americans is 56 percent of the median white American family income.

Starting in the 1970s, changes to the economy and to public policy began concentrating a larger and larger share of national income in the pockets of the richest members of society. Incomes for the middle class and the poor have hardly grown at all, while incomes for the richest 1 percent almost tripled.

These changes to the income distribution mean that as more African Americans succeed in overcoming the many obstacles to reaching the middle class, the payoff is not as great as it had been for social groups that climbed the income ladder earlier in U.S. history. To see this, consider the income earned at the 35th percentile, where the median African American stood in 2016. In 1968, a person at the 35th percentile had an income 69 percent of the national mean. But by 2016, income at the 35th percentile had fallen to be just 49 percent of the national mean. Because of rising income inequality, successfully reaching the middle of the income distribution did not provide the same economic reward to blacks as it had to previous groups of Americans.

The effect of rising income inequality on racial disparities also becomes evident by simulating what the income gap would look like if the overall income distribution had stayed constant. If overall inequality hadn't gone up, the ratio of median black family income to white family income would have climbed from 57 percent to 70 percent, decreasing the racial income gap by 30 percent. That would still be a far cry from racial economic equality, of course. Racial discrimination, residential segregation, neighborhood disinvestment, and other remnants of America's long history of racial subjugation would all still be present even if overall economic inequality hadn't gotten worse. But this simulation shows that in a world where our country's growth were shared more equitably, we would have a substantially smaller racial income gap than we see today.

Of course, rising inequality has hurt Americans of all races—even for whites, the median income has declined by 14 percent as a share of the national mean over the past five decades. But because African Americans remain overrepresented among the poorer segments of society, economic shifts that have harmed almost everyone have also increased the average income gap between blacks and whites. These shifts were strong enough to undo what would otherwise have been substantial—though far from complete—progress toward racial equity in income.

These findings demonstrate how economic inequality and racial inequality are fundamentally intertwined. Over the past 50 years, a fairly large improvement in the relative position of African Americans was entirely undone by national economic shifts. Going forward, high levels of overall inequality will make it harder to achieve racial parity since any improvement in relative terms means less in terms of dollars.

Yet this analysis also shows how policies to make the economy more equal in general can contribute to greater equality between races—a point many civil rights leaders and academics have made over the years. The vast majority of Americans have an interest in reversing wage stagnation and making the economy more equitable. This offers a second front in the battle for racial equality. Efforts to reduce discrimination, equalize access to education, ensure equal treatment by the legal system, and otherwise end racial stratification should continue since they seem to be making real, if slow, progress. But these policies should be paired with broader economic policies to end wage stagnation for Americans of all races and, in so doing, reduce the gaps between racial groups.

EVALUATING THE AUTHOR'S ARGUMENTS:

In this viewpoint, author Robert Manduca argues that increasing income inequality has been especially hard on African Americans. Should race be considered in discussions of economic inequality? Why or why not? How might civil rights movements and economic equality movements support each other? Are there ways they might undermine each other's goals?

Women Suffer More from Income Inequality

"Men make up an overwhelming majority of top earners across the U.S. economy, even though women now represent almost half of the country's workforce."

Inequality.org

In the following viewpoint, Inequality.org explores gender and income inequality. Women make up a disproportional percent of low-wage workers. They make up an extremely small percent of high-wage workers, such as corporate CEOs (chief executive officers). This means that women on average earn less than men. In addition, they may do far more unpaid work, such as child care. Women tend to hold more college debt and have less retirement savings. That makes the wealth gap between men and women even higher than the income gap. The gap increases between white men and women of color. Transgender people also suffer, and transgender people of color are the worst off. Inequality.org tracks inequality-related news and views. It is sponsored by the Institute for Policy Studies, a progressive think tank.

AS YOU READ, CONSIDER THE FOLLOWING QUESTIONS:
1. How does income inequality affect women of color in the United States?
2. How does the US gender pay gap compare to other countries?
3. How can the gender pay gap affect women when they retire?

The global trend towards extreme wealth and income concentration has dramatically strengthened the economic and political power of those individuals—overwhelmingly male—at the top. In the United States and around the world, women continue to be underrepresented in high-level, highly paid positions and overrepresented in low-paying jobs. Women of color and transgender individuals experience particularly high levels of poverty, unemployment, and other economic hardships. Gender discrimination and sexual harassment in the workplace contribute significantly to these persistent economic divides.

Gender Income Gaps

Female-dominated occupations—such as childcare and restaurant service—continue to occupy the lower rungs of the U.S. wage ladder. Women make up 63 percent of workers earning the federal minimum wage, a wage rate stuck at $7.25 since 2009. By contrast, women represent only 5 percent of CEOs at Fortune 500 firms. CEOs took home $13.1 million on average in 2016.

White males particularly dominate highly lucrative financial industry jobs. At the top five U.S. investment banks (JPMorgan Chase, Goldman Sachs, Bank of America Merrill Lynch, Morgan Stanley, and Citigroup), males make up from 69 to 82 percent executives and top managers. The share who are white ranges from 78 to 87 percent. More than two-thirds of all New York City securities industry employees were male in 2016, and nearly two-thirds were white.

Men make up an overwhelming majority of top earners across the U.S. economy, even though women now represent almost half of the country's workforce. Women comprise just 27 percent of the top 10 percent, and their share of higher income groups runs even

Organized to raise awareness about the gender pay gap, Equal Pay Day is the symbolic day in a year when women's earnings would catch up to men's earnings from the previous year.

smaller. Among the top 1 percent, women make up slightly less than 17 percent of workers, while at the top 0.1 percent level, they make up only 11 percent.

Other major economies show similar trend lines. A study of eight high-income countries found that women made up just 14 percent to 22 percent of the top 1 percent of earners. These surveys were conducted during the 2010-2014 period. The U.S. figure is from 2012.

Throughout the U.S. workforce, women remain vastly underpaid. Among full-time workers, women earned less than 81 cents for every dollar a man earned in 2016. If part-time workers were included, the gap would be even wider, since women are more likely to work reduced schedules, often in order to manage childrearing and other caregiving work.

Within racial groups, the largest pay gaps between men and women appear among whites and Asians—not because Latinas and black women have made faster progress towards equity but because average pay for men in these groups falls far below the compensation of white and Asian men.

American women earn less than men, on average, in all industries. The largest pay gaps are in management positions, where men made $88,000 on average in 2016, compared to just $55,000 for women. The smallest gap appears in the construction sector, but women make up only 9 percent of workers in this industry.

The U.S. gender pay gap, while unacceptably large, is not the world's widest. But accurately measuring these gaps across countries can be difficult. Within the OECD group of higher-income nations, South Korea holds the widest gap, with men earning 37 percent more than women, on average. The country with the narrowest gap: Luxembourg, where men make just 3.4 percent more than women. Gaps have been smallest in OECD countries where the share of workers covered by collective bargaining agreements hits at least 80 percent and widest in countries with weak collective bargaining and no or very low minimum wages.

The International Labor Organization concedes that more work needs to be done to develop more accurate global gender gap analyses. One factor skewing the numbers: Women do considerably more unpaid work, from housekeeping to caring for children and the elderly. Among the 21 countries reporting data for at least one year during the 2013-2015 period, the West Bank and Gaza had the greatest imbalance, with men devoting just 16 percent as much time to unpaid domestic and caregiving work as women. Belgium, where men spend 63 percent as much time on these activities as women, ranked at the top.

In the UK, a new regulation requires corporations to disclose the pay gaps between their male and female employees. Financial firms have among the largest divides because of the scarcity of women in top positions. In 2018, HSBC reported the biggest gap, with the bank's female employees averaging just 41 percent as much as UK male employees. For all 10,000 firms in the survey, the median-paid male employee received 9.7 percent more in pay than the median female.

Gender Wealth Gaps

Most inequality analysis focuses on income (the wages earned from a job or from capital gains) rather than wealth (the sum of one's assets minus debts). Income inequality, while stark, pales in comparison to wealth inequality. The divides become even more dramatic when viewed through a gender lens.

At the top end, we have no more striking sign of increasing global wealth concentration than the rise of the billionaire class. The number of individuals with fortunes worth at least $1 billion more than doubled between 2010 and 2018, while remaining overwhelmingly male. In 2018, only 256 women ranked among the world's 2,208 billionaires. Seventy-seven hail from the United States, more than double the number in any other country.

One important component of wealth, retirement savings, shows an even wider gap between men and women. According to the Transamerica Center for Retirement Studies, American women in 2017 held $42,000 in median retirement savings, compared to $123,000 for men. Some 21 percent of women and 12 percent of men have less than $10,000 in retirement accounts. Both pension plan and Social Security payouts reflect in part past earnings. The gender pay gap means women end up with fewer post-retirement resources. In 2017, the $15,000 average annual Social Security benefit for women lagged the benefit for men by $4,000. The smaller retirement nest eggs of women also have to stretch further than male retirement savings, simply because women have longer life expectancies.

Debt also significantly impacts wealth. Crushing student loan burdens drag many young Americans far into the negative side of the wealth line, with the heaviest for female students. Women comprise 56 percent of college students, but hold nearly two-thirds of outstanding student loan debt.

According to the American Association of University Women, black women graduate with the most debt—$30,400, on average—compared to $22,000 for white women and $19,500 for white men.

Gender Poverty Gaps

The gender poverty gap widened over the past 50 years. In 1968, 10.8 percent of women aged 18-64 (6.1 million women) and 7.2 percent of men (3.7 million) in this age group lived below the poverty line. In 2016, 13.4 percent of women in this age group (13.4 million women) were living in poverty, compared to 9.7 percent of adult men (9.4 million men). The poverty threshold for a single person in 2016: $11,880 in annual income. Households led by single women with children had a poverty rate of 35.6 percent, more than twice the 17.3 percent rate for households led by single men with children, according to the National Women's Law Center.

Poverty is a particularly acute problem for women of color, affecting 21.4 percent of Black women, 18.7 percent of Latinas, and 22.8 percent of Native American women, compared to the national poverty rate for white men of 7.0 percent.

Transgender Economic Gaps

Transgender Americans experience poverty at double the rate of the general population, and transgender people of color experience even higher rates. The National Center for Transgender Equality has found that 43 percent of Latino, 41 percent of Native American, 40 percent of multiracial, and 38 percent of Black transgender respondents lived in poverty in 2015.

In 2015, the overall unemployment rate for transgender Americans stood at 15 percent, compared to 5 percent for the general population. The unemployment rate ran even higher for American Indian, Black, Latino, Middle Eastern, and multi-racial transgender Americans.

Income Inequality Is Bad for Your Health

"Many health outcomes—everything from life expectancy to infant mortality and obesity—can be linked to the level of economic inequality."

Inequality.org

In the following viewpoint, Inequality.org explores the effect of income inequality on health. People in poverty often have worse health and live shorter lives. Poor families have higher levels of stress, obesity, and smoking, which can lead to health problems. They may also struggle to get adequate health care. This leads to a dramatic difference in life expectancy between poor Americans and rich ones. Moreover, inequality affects health for everyone, even people who are well-off. Researchers say this may be because inequality leads to more stress, fear, and insecurity for everyone. Inequality.org tracks inequality-related news and views. It is sponsored by the Institute for Policy Studies, a progressive think tank.

AS YOU READ, CONSIDER THE FOLLOWING QUESTIONS:
1. How does income inequality relate to heart health?
2. How does income inequality relate to the survival rate of babies?
3. How does income inequality affect mental health?

How do inequality and health relate? Increasing evidence from scientists the world over indicates that many health outcomes—everything from life expectancy to infant mortality and obesity—can be linked to the level of economic inequality within a given population. Greater economic inequality appears to lead to worse health outcomes.

By greater inequality, epidemiologists—the scientists who study the health of populations—don't just mean poverty. Poor health and poverty do go hand-in-hand. But high levels of inequality, the epidemiological research shows, negatively affect the health of even the affluent, mainly because, researchers contend, inequality reduces social cohesion, a dynamic that leads to more stress, fear, and insecurity for everyone.

Cross-National Comparisons

Economists and health experts have known for years that people who live in poorer societies live shorter lives. But research also points to an additional factor in explaining life expectancy: a society's level of inequality. People live longer in nations with lower levels of inequality, as measured here by the Gini coefficient, a standard global benchmark. In the United States, average life expectancy is four years shorter than in some of the most equitable countries.

A study published in the *Journal of the American College of Cardiology* in 2019 found that the higher the level of income inequality, the higher the rate of cardiovascular-related deaths and hospitalizations. Based on surveys from 2009 to 2015, participating countries with the lowest levels of income inequality (Central Europe and Scandinavian countries), had the lowest heart failure rate, at 10.9 per 100 person-years. Countries with intermediate income inequality levels (North America, Australia, and India) had a rate of 11.7 per 100 person-years, while those with the highest level of inequality had the highest rates of heart failure, at 13.7 per 100 person-years.

In 2017, nations with the smallest income gaps between households at the 90th and 10th percentiles had significantly fewer infant deaths than other nations. A household at the 90th percentile has more income than 90 percent of households. The United States is at

Imbalances in income and wealth are associated with poor health. Some nonprofits aim to correct that by reaching out to impoverished Americans and those in areas with no access to health care.

the extreme end among other industrialized countries, with the largest gap between the rich and the rest of the population and by far the worst infant mortality rate, at 5.7 per 1,000 live births, compared to just 1.6 per 1,000 in Iceland.

Extreme inequality appears to affect how people perceive their well-being. In nations where the top 1 percent hold a greater share of national income, people tend to have a lower sense of personal well-being. Researchers are also finding links between inequality and mental health. Countries with larger rich-poor gaps have a higher risk of schizophrenia incidences. In general, a 0.2 point increase in a country's Gini coefficient results in eight additional incidences of schizophrenia per 100,000 people. Researchers believe that higher inequality undercuts social cohesion and capital and increases chronic stress.

Inequality and Health in the United States

The same association between high economic inequality and poor health can be observed within the United States.

Advocates for raising the retirement age for collecting Social Security benefits often base their argument on rising U.S. life expectancy. But a landmark study published in 2016 found that low-income Americans—those who depend most on Social Security—have not been part of this positive trend. The divergence is most stark among men. In 2014, those in the top 5 percent of household income could expect to celebrate their 88th birthday, an increase of three years since 2001. For those in the bottom 5 percent, life expectancy has essentially flatlined at around 76 years.

The life expectancy divide is widest among the very richest and poorest in U.S. society. Men in the top 1 percent of the income distribution can now expect to live 15 years longer than those in the bottom 1 percent. For women, the difference is about 10 years—an effect equivalent to that of a lifetime of smoking.

Within the United States, people live longer in the more equal states. In Hawaii, which has relatively equitable income distribution, people can expect to live nearly seven years longer than in highly unequal Mississippi.

In the 1970s, death rates from all cancer types were similar in rich and poor U.S. counties. As inequality has increased across the nation, this has changed. Today, rich counties have significantly lower levels of cancer deaths than poor counties. Lung cancer deaths in low-income counties have actually increased, from 41.2 per 100,000 per year to 47.7, while dropping slightly in the higher-income counties.

U.S. households with annual incomes below $50,000 report higher levels of stress than other families. Average stress levels gradually declined after the 2007-2008 financial crisis, but the stress gap between rich and poor households has been increasing. Blue collar and low-income jobs are often more stressful and physically demanding than white collar jobs. This contributes to a variety of other health problems, such as high blood pressure, back problems, and diabetes. Societal forces, such as discrimination based on race, gender, and sexual orientation, add to the stress level of certain population groups.

On average, women in the United States have lower rates of obesity as their income rises. Those with household incomes above

350 percent of the federal poverty line have obesity rates of 29.7 percent, compared to 45.2 percent for incomes less than 130 percent of the federal poverty line. In addition to higher stress levels, factors such as food deserts and lack of recreational facilities in poor communities contribute to higher obesity rates among low-income women. Among men, obe-

sity rates are similar across income groups, while male college graduates have a significantly lower rate than those with less education.

U.S. smoking rates vary widely by income group, from 12.1 percent in households earning more than $100,000 per year to 32.2 percent in households earning less than $20,000 per year. In addition to higher stress levels, low-income communities face heavier targeting by tobacco corporations, both through advertising and high concentrations of stores that sell cigarettes.

The lower American workers rank on the national economic ladder, the more likely their jobs will be physically demanding. Such jobs can lead to more stress, both physical and mental—and higher medical bills. Workers in physically demanding jobs such as janitorial, maintenance, and housekeeping positions, also typically retire earlier, before they can claim full Social Security benefits.

The bottom third of U.S. earners tend to retire earlier than other Americans, in part because their jobs are often more physically demanding. Because American workers cannot claim full retirement benefits before age 66, this trend exacerbates economic inequality among seniors.

Chapter 2

What Are the Effects of Income Inequality?

Despite the Equal Pay Act, women earn 80 cents for every dollar paid to men.

Income Inequality Isn't the Problem

David R. Henderson

"Entrepreneurial innovation that improves the lives of consumers is good; using political pull to transfer wealth is bad."

In the following viewpoint, David R. Henderson argues that economic inequality is often misunderstood. He states that wealth inequality does not necessarily hurt people with less wealth. In fact, a new invention may benefit the inventor by giving them more wealth, and it also may benefit the public by giving them access to the invention. The author also notes that worldwide poverty has been falling in recent decades, because people in the poorest countries are doing better. In his view, we should encourage policies that lead to higher economic growth, regardless of how much they benefit the wealthiest people. David R. Henderson is an economist and author.

AS YOU READ, CONSIDER THE FOLLOWING QUESTIONS:

1. How can an event that increases wealth inequality benefit everyone, according to the examples in this viewpoint?
2. What is the difference between good economic inequality and bad, according to the author?
3. Why has worldwide extreme poverty fallen?

"Income Inequality Isn't the Problem," by David R. Henderson, The Board of Trustees of Leland Stanford Junior University, February 20, 2018. Reprinted by permission.

If you've been paying attention to economic controversies in the last decade, you may have noticed many discussions about economic inequality. It's a hot topic and several people believe that the alleviation of poverty requires a substantial reduction in inequality. For example, Thomas Piketty, the French economist whose book *Capital in the Twenty-First Century* became a bestseller, understands the distinction between income inequality and poverty but sometimes uses the terms interchangeably, as if one necessarily begets the other. But inequality of income and wealth can remain high or even increase while poverty is decreasing.

In order to understand economic inequality, we need to ask a few questions. First, are there good kinds of economic inequality and bad kinds? Second, is it a good idea, as many policymakers and even some economists insist, to reduce inequality by taxing those at the top end more heavily? Third, has poverty been increasing? Fourth has economic inequality been increasing?

To answer the first question, let us consider two historical figures of twentieth-century American history. The first came to prominence in the late 1940s, when he invented a light one-man chainsaw, and sold more than 100,000 of them at a price that made him quite rich. That added slightly to wealth inequality. But although the wealth gap between this man, inventor Robert McCulloch, and his customers was higher than it was before, the customers got a product they valued that made their lives easier. In economists' terms, the wealth of these customers increased slightly. Is that increase in wealth inequality a problem? When I've asked college students this question, the vast majority says no—and I agree.

Now let's consider the second figure. In the early 1940s, as a Congressman from Texas, this man defended the budget of the Federal Communications Commission when a more senior member of the House of Representatives was trying to cut it. So the FCC owed him a favor. One FCC official suggested the politician have his wife apply for a license for a radio station in the underserved Austin market. She did so and within a few weeks, the FCC granted her permission to buy the license from the current owners. She then applied for permission to increase its time of operation from daylight-hours-only to 24 hours a day and at a much better part of the

The author of this viewpoint notes that poverty is on the decline and suggests taking a deeper look at economic inequality.

AM spectrum—and the FCC granted her permission within a few weeks. The commission also prevented competitors from entering the Austin market.

These moves made Lyndon Johnson and his wife very rich. When he ran for President in 1964, the radio station accounted for over half of his $14-million net worth. This increase in his wealth added slightly to wealth inequality. But customers in the Austin market were, due to the FCC restrictions on further radio stations, slightly less well off than if more stations had been allowed. When I tell this story to college audiences and ask them if they think there's an important difference between McCulloch's and Johnson's methods of increasing wealth inequality, virtually all of them do, and few will defend the latter way.

How does this relate to wealth inequality? In any given year, there isn't just one inventor or innovator. There are thousands. So each one's success increases wealth inequality a little but also improves the well-being of tens of millions of people who are less wealthy. Also, as other competitors enter the market and compete with the innovator, they drive down prices and make consumers even better off. Indeed,

Yale University economist William D. Nordhaus has estimated that only 2.2 percent of the gains from innovation are captured by the innovators. Most of the rest goes to consumers.

In short, there is indeed a distinction between good economic inequality and bad. Entrepreneurial innovation that improves the lives of consumers is good; using political pull to transfer wealth is bad.

Consider another example—two of the richest people in the world are Bill Gates and Carlos Slim. Gates got rich by starting and building Microsoft, whose main product, an operating system for personal computers, made life better for the rest of us. Would you have a well-functioning personal computer if Bill Gates hadn't existed? Yes. But his existence and his clear thinking early on hastened the PC revolution by at least a year. That might not sound like a lot, but each gain we consumers got from each step of the PC revolution occurred a year earlier because of Bill Gates. Over 40 years, that amounts to trillions of dollars in value to consumers. The market value of Microsoft is currently just shy of $700 billion. Assume that Microsoft was much better than other innovators at capturing consumer value and captured fully 10 percent of the value it created, rather than the usual 2.2 percent. That means it has created almost $7 trillion of value for consumers over those forty years.

Mexican multi-billionaire Carlos Slim is currently the seventh-richest man in the world. He got rich the way Lyndon Johnson got rich. The Mexican government handed him a monopoly on telecommunications in Mexico and he uses it to charge high prices for phone calls. Slim is clearly exacerbating income inequality in a way that makes other people poorer.

Thomas Piketty concedes that it matters how one gets rich, and that many rich people made their money legitimately. But when it comes to advocating policy, he forgets that important distinction. He advocates an annual "global tax on capital" with rates that would rise with wealth. "One might imagine," he writes, "a rate of 0 percent for net assets below 1 million euros, 1 percent between 1 million and 5 million, and 2 percent above 5 million." He adds, "one might prefer" a stiff annual tax of "5 or 10 percent on assets above 1 billion euros."

But such a policy doesn't discriminate between those who accrued their wealth honestly and in ways that ultimately contributed to the social welfare and those who got rich through government power. Here's Piketty's response to that point: "In any case, the courts cannot resolve every case of ill-gotten gains or unjustified wealth. A tax on capital would be a less blunt and more systematic instrument for dealing with the question."

Piketty's last sentence is the opposite of the truth. A tax on capital, no matter whether that capital was acquired legitimately or illegitimately, is incredibly blunt. It's systematic only in the sense that it systematically takes wealth from all wealthy people. I agree with Piketty that courts are not usually the ideal way to resolve the issue of ill-gotten gains: much of what government does to produce those gains is legal, however morally questionable. The best way to prevent ill-gotten gains is to take away the government's power to grant them. If the Mexican government had not had the power to create a telecommunications monopoly, for example, Slim's wealth would be—much slimmer.

That brings us to the second question: Is it a good idea to reduce inequality by more heavily taxing those at the top end? If there's anything we know from basic economics, it's that incentives affect behavior. Tax high incomes or wealth heavily and you will have fewer people trying to make high incomes and get wealthy. Moreover, even if the incentive effect were slight, high taxes on highly productive people take wealth out of their hands, where much of it likely would have been used to finance more pro-consumer innovation and productivity, and put it in the hands of government bureaucracies. That simple transfer of wealth, independent of the effect on incentives, makes a society worse off.

Third, has poverty been increasing? No. In fact, what economists call extreme poverty—living on an income of less than $1.90 a day—has fallen dramatically over the last 3 decades. For the first time in world history, fewer than one billion people live in extreme poverty.

This is all the more striking when you remember that the world population, at 7.6 billion people, is at an all-time high. Why has this happened? Because of increased international trade and economic growth—which have made some people extremely wealthy, while also lifting over one billion others out of crippling destitution. The argument that economic inequality somehow exacerbates poverty is specious.

Finally, has economic inequality been increasing or decreasing? The wrong way to answer that question is by comparing the wealth of billionaires to the wealth of the poorest people on earth. The correct way

is to compute something called the Gini coefficient. This coefficient, which can range from 0 to 1, measures income inequality. With total income equality, the Gini would be 0; with total inequality, which would mean one person having all the world's income, the Gini would be 1. So what has happened to the Gini coefficient over time? Economists Tomas Hellebrandt and Paolo Mauro reported the answer in a 2015 study for the Peterson Institute for International Economics. They found that between 2003 and 2013, the worldwide Gini coefficient fell from 0.69 to 0.65, indicating reduced income inequality. Moreover, the two economists predict that by 2035, income inequality will decline further, with the Gini coefficient falling to 0.61. The reason is not that higher income people will do worse but that lower income people in some of the poorest countries, like India and China, will do much better because of economic growth.

If the problem we care about is poverty, then the calls to tax the rich and reduce income inequality are misguided. Instead, we should be cheering for policies that lead to higher economic growth. One other important measure is increased immigration. Allowing more immigration into the United States would allow people to move from low-productivity jobs in poor countries to higher-productivity jobs in America. That would dramatically improve the plight of the poor while also improving, but by a smaller margin, the well-being of the rich. Piketty, for all his faults, put his finger on how to do so. He wrote: "A seemingly more peaceful form of redistribution and regulation of global wealth inequality is immigration. Rather than move capital, which poses all sorts of difficulties, it is sometimes simpler to allow labor to move to places where wages are higher."

Amen, frère.

EVALUATING THE AUTHOR'S ARGUMENTS:

In this viewpoint, author David R. Henderson argues that letting people become very wealthy benefits everyone. Do you agree with his explanation? If so, what, if anything, should the government do about income inequality? Compare this to Chapter 1, Viewpoint 2, which argues that most wealthy people make their wealth by investing money they already have. Can the two views be reconciled?

Viewpoint

2

Overcome Inequality by Offering More Credit

"Inequality is preventing people with less income and wealth from reaching their potential in terms of education and invention."

Chris Doucouliagos

In the following viewpoint, Chris Doucouliagos argues that income inequality keeps people from becoming entrepreneurs. In turn, this can hurt the economy. The author uses data from the OECD, the Organisation for Economic Co-operation and Development, to make his point. The OECD has 36 member countries, including the United States and many European countries. The author claims that better access to credit would allow low-income earners to improve their lives. This, in turn, should improve the economy. Chris Doucouliagos is a professor in the Department of Economics at Deakin Business School in Australia.

AS YOU READ, CONSIDER THE FOLLOWING QUESTIONS:
1. How do advances in technology affect the economy?
2. How can unions help, or hurt, the economy, according to the author?
3. How can access to credit help low-income earners and improve the economy?

Aworld where a few people have most of the wealth motivates others who are poor to strive to earn more. And when they do, they'll invest in businesses and other areas of the economy. That's the argument for inequality. But it's wrong.

Our study of 21 OECD countries over more than 100 years shows income inequality actually restricts people from earning more, educating themselves and becoming entrepreneurs. That flows on to businesses who in turn invest less in things like plant and equipment.

Inequality makes it harder for economies to benefit from innovation. However, if people have access to credit or the money to move up, it can offset this effect.

We measured the impact of this by looking at the number of patents for new inventions and then also looking at the Gini coefficient and the income share of the top 10%. The Gini coefficient is a measure of the distribution of income or wealth within a nation.

How Inequality Reduces Innovation

From 1870 to 1977, inequality measured by the Gini coefficient fell by about 40%. During this time people actually got more innovative and productivity increased, incomes also increased.

But inequality has increased in recent decades and it's having the opposite effect.

Inequality is preventing people with less income and wealth from reaching their potential in terms of education and invention. There's also less entrepreneurship.

Inequality also means the market for new goods shrinks. One study shows that if incomes are more equal among people, people who are less well off, buy more. Having this larger market for new products, incentivises companies to create new things to sell.

If wealth is concentrated among only a small group of people, it actually increases demand for imported luxuries and handmade products. In contrast to this, distributed incomes means more mass produced goods are manufactured.

What's been driving inequality since the 1980s is changes to economies—countries trading more with each other and advances in technology. As this happens old products and industries fade while new ones take their place.

Does seeing the 1 percent thrive motivate the 99 percent to innovate and invest in the economy? Research shows the opposite. Income inequality actually stifles entrepreneurship.

These changes have delivered significant net benefits to society. Reducing trade and innovation will only make everyone poorer.

The declining number of people in unions has also contributed to inequality, as workers lose collective bargaining power and some rights. At the same time, unions can adversely affect innovation within firms.

Unions discourage innovation when they resist the adoption of new technology in the workplace. Also, if innovation creates profits for firms but some of these are taken up by higher wages (lobbied for by unions), these reduced profits provide less incentive for firms to innovate.

Where workers' jobs are protected, for example with union membership, there's often less resistance to innovation and technological change.

Giving People Access to Credit Could Change This

Most countries have much higher levels of inequality than the OECD average. This combination of high inequality and low financial development is a major obstacle to economic prosperity.

When financial markets work well, everyone gets access to the amount of credit they can afford and can invest as much as they need. We found that for a nation with a credit-to-GDP ratio of more than 108%, low income earners are less discouraged by not having a share of the wealth. There's less of a dampening effect on innovation.

Unfortunately, most countries (including many in the OECD) are far from this threshold. In 2016, the credit-to-GDP ratio averaged 56% across all countries, and only 28% for the least developed. Until 2005, Australia was also below this threshold.

This means governments should look at providing more people with more access to credit, especially to the poor, to stimulate growth.

For financially developed nations like Australia, increased inequality actually has less of an effect on innovation and growth. So tackling inequality might not be as easy as increasing access to credit.

Spending and taxing are already historically high and growing inequality makes it harder to further raise taxes. Countries like Australia are not unequal societies in the sense of having significant barriers to people improving their income.

Australia is a relatively egalitarian nation. In 2016, the top 1% owned 22% of the wealth in Australia, compared to 42% in the USA, and 74% in Russia.

Governments in more developed nations can instead try to maintain a stable financial sector to improve growth or by training and education.

Invest in Education

Stephen Bell

"The failure to reasonably share income and educational opportunities is creating a highly volatile mix of unhappy 'losers'."

In the following viewpoint, Stephen Bell debates the link between inequality and economic growth. One standard economic theory is the supply-side theory. It claims that the best way to create economic growth is to lower taxes and decrease regulation. The author argues that demand is more important than supply. In economies that have a lot of inequality, demand for goods drops. Poor people can't afford to buy a lot, and rich people don't consume enough to make up for their small percentage of the population. The author argues that rising inequality is weakening economic growth in developed countries. Stephen Bell is a professor of political economy at the University of Queensland in Australia.

AS YOU READ, CONSIDER THE FOLLOWING QUESTIONS:

1. What has been happening to economic growth in the Western world, according to the viewpoint?
2. When wage increases mainly go to the top earners, how does that affect the demand for goods?
3. What does the author think the government should do to promote economic growth?

In the last decade or more, economic growth has slowed across the Western world, although a belated though weak recovery has been under way since around 2017. In the US, for example, growth in gross output per capita averages around 1% a year this century. That's about half the average rate during the second half of the 20th century.

American economist Arthur Okun famously argued there was a trade-off between equality and economic efficiency, implying little chance of high inequality and sluggish economic growth occurring together. Yet this is exactly what is happening in the US. What has gone wrong?

In *The Captured Economy*, Brink Lindsey and Steven Teles explore US economic sectors such as finance, land use, occupational licensing and intellectual property rights. They argue powerful interests have captured these sectors and are using the state to distort markets to their advantage. This kind of rent-seeking is weakening growth and driving up inequality. As the authors put it:

> *Across a number of sectors, the US economy has become less open to competition and more clogged by insider-protecting deals … Those deals make our economy less dynamic and innovative, leading to slower economic growth … At the same time, they redistribute income and wealth upwards to elites in a position to exploit the political system to their favour.*

This special dealing is but one facet of a much wider problem of competing claims for economic resources increasingly damaging Western economies. The arguments by Lindsey and Teles concern dysfunctions on the supply side of the economy.

In our recent book, *Fair Share: Competing Claims and Australia's Economic Future*, Michael Keating and I argue that even bigger competing claims and distributional problems are now affecting the demand side of Western economies. These problems are also producing weak economic growth and rising inequality.

Time to Pay Attention to Demand

But how are these two outcomes connected? In *Fair Share*, we argue that rising inequality is weakening economic growth across the

Since the 1980s, wages have increased for top earners in the United States but have largely stagnated for others in the labor force.

advanced economies by reducing aggregate demand. Our account differs from mainstream economics, which argues that growth stems mainly from the supply side of the economy.

In recent decades many neoliberal, supply-side policies have been implemented. The recent sluggish pattern of growth calls the supply-side theory into question. Indeed, the gap between theory and reality has prompted former US treasury secretary Lawrence Summers to argue that "the events of the last decade should precipitate a crisis in the field of macroeconomics."

Some salient facts on the demand side are increasingly hard to ignore. Most Western economies have been marked by increased inequality since the 1980s. Wage shares have fallen.

Even more important has been the rise in income inequality. The wage increases that have occurred have been largely concentrated among the top income earners. These "winners" have a lower propensity to consume than those in the lower deciles of earnings distribution. As a result, too much income inequality and slow wages growth relative to productivity growth risk a continuing shortfall in demand and hence weaker economic growth.

Prior to the Global Financial Crisis (GFC), many economic policies sought to avoid this shortfall in aggregate demand. This did so either by maintaining a very competitive exchange rate to support export-led growth (e.g. China, Germany) or, more often, by increasing the availability of consumer credit to support consumer demand (e.g. the US, UK).

Neither of these strategies has proved viable in the longer run. First, not all countries can be net exporters at the same time. Second, the required growth in consumer credit became increasingly risky, and eventually helped fuel the GFC.

Since then, the advanced economies have experienced protracted stagnation and a weak recovery due to a shortfall in aggregate demand. The longer this shortfall continues, the greater the risk that the rate of increase in potential output will also slow.

The impact on economic output is due to lack of new investment, on which technological progress depends, and atrophying of workforce skills when labour is not fully employed. Indeed, the combination of low unemployment and slow economic growth suggests this slowdown in potential output growth is already occurring in the US.

More generally, however, competing economic claims can potentially deliver various combinations of inflation, wage stagnation, growing inequality, weak demand and slower economic growth. Our central proposition in Fair Share links income distribution and economic growth.

Why Growth Depends on Balanced Distribution

Western capitalism has always run on a fairly narrow distributional path. If the distributional balance gets too far out of kilter in either direction the threats of inadequate aggregate demand and weak growth are likely to emerge.

As we saw in the 1970s, pursuit of excessive wage increases risks stagflation, resulting in inadequate investment and rising unemployment. On the other hand, and as is happening now, a significant shift towards wage stagnation and increased income inequality risks slower growth through inadequate demand and consumption.

Hence, it is the distributional shifts, in pursuit of higher wages in the 1970s and more recently in favour of capital and the highest-income groups, that have largely been responsible for the difficulties in both epochs in maintaining growth in the advanced capitalist economies.

Our theory thus suggests that the problems of stagflation in the 1970s were not as far removed from today's problems as one might think. The root cause of the problems across both eras has essentially been distributional changes.

Some analysts argue that regulatory and other changes have altered the relative power of those involved in competing claims, with workers and wage levels, in particular, losing out. Others, such as Lindsay and Teles, argue returns are skewed by oligopolistic competition, rent-seeking and other forms of market power and powerlessness (see also Cameron Murray and Paul Frijters' *Games of Mates* on Australia).

We acknowledge both of these changes but argue that the biggest changes in income distribution have come from technological changes that have hollowed out middle-income jobs, while any relative labour shortages have tended to be skill-biased. These two factors are the main drivers of increased income polarisation.

Furthermore, to the extent that trade-union power matters, we think changes in the industrial and occupational structure of the workforce, in response to technological change, have largely been responsible for reduced trade union membership and the loss of bargaining power.

What Should Governments Do About This?

In response, governments should aim to boost wages and redress growing income inequality. Any such strategy will be most effective if it focuses on responding to the technological changes that are the prime cause of rising inequality. As Thomas Piketty concluded in the most significant analysis of inequality published this century:

> *To sum up: the best way to increase wages and reduce wage inequalities in the long run is to invest in education and skills.*

We argue therefore that education and training need to be boosted to help workers cope with changing markets and job opportunities. This approach can be expected to boost both aggregate demand and supply. Direct measures to boost lower incomes may also be needed to improve the social safety net for those who miss out.

More generally, the successful continuation of the open-economy model, and indeed the sustainability of capitalist democracy, will depend upon the successful resolution of competing claims. In particular, this requires a fair sharing of the gains from increased economic production and a tight link between wages and productivity growth.

It is certainly clear that the supply-side, neoliberal policies of recent decades have largely run their course in many advanced economies. Too often the starting premise of the supply-side agenda is that the role of government should be minimised through further deregulation and tax cuts. However, the nature of many of today's problems requires government to be more interventionist rather than less, while still maintaining the key strengths of an open, liberal, market economy.

The new focus of policy must be on the demand side. The failure to reasonably share income and educational opportunities is creating a highly volatile mix of unhappy "losers". Hence, we see a growing political backlash, the rise of right-wing populism and extremism, Brexit, Trump etc.

The backlash against globalisation and economic restructuring is real and growing. It poses a threat to economic development and to liberal democratic capitalism.

[...]

A new agenda is needed. We have to recognise that economic growth inevitably involves economic transformation, based on innovation and technological change. Thus, contrary to the assumptions many economists make, it is highly probable that economic growth will impact on the distribution of incomes. This of itself can create future problems for the sustainability of that growth.

The bottom line, economically and politically, is that governments need to be prepared to promote demand as well as supply. Increasingly, we can no longer escape the distributional issues at hand. The winners will need to help the losers through more effective support and a degree of redistribution—especially if things get worse through ongoing wage stagnation and rising resistance to the perceived inequities of the present economic system.

EVALUATING THE AUTHOR'S ARGUMENTS:

Viewpoint author Stephen Bell argues that government should invest in education and job training. Based on what you have learned so far, would this successfully address some or all of the problems of wealth inequality? Be sure to consider the questions of race and gender introduced in Chapter 1, Viewpoints 4 and 5.

Fight Poverty, Not Inequality

Manuel Hinds

"Inequality is the mechanism that will spread the benefits of the new knowledge society across the entire world."

In the following viewpoint, author Manuel Hinds argues against statements made by Joseph Stiglitz, a recipient of the Nobel Prize in Economic Sciences, regarding inequality. Hinds addresses four of Stiglitz's claims in turn. He then states that the problem is poverty rather than inequality. To illustrate this, he notes that it is not a problem if one person makes $200,000 per year and someone else makes 366 times that. However, it is a problem if the person making $200,000 per year makes 366 times more than their neighbor. Their neighbor would be destitute. While the inequality is the same in both cases, one example leaves a person in poverty and the other does not. Manuel Hinds is the former finance minister of El Salvador. He has also worked with the World Bank.

AS YOU READ, CONSIDER THE FOLLOWING QUESTIONS:
1. What does the author mean what he claims that arguments about inequality have become moralistic?
2. How can inequality generate innovation, which in turn generates opportunities, according to the author?
3. What is the current state of education in the United States, according to the viewpoint?

The growing inequality of wealth and income has become a hot topic in the last few years in the United States, attracting both moral condemnations and radical recommendations aiming at reversing it. According to the most popular quotation, the top 1% of the population of the United States controls 40% of the country's wealth and 25% of its income.

In a 2011 Vanity Fair article (Of the 1%, by the 1%, for the 1%), and in a book (*The Price of Inequality*), Nobel Prize winner Joseph Stiglitz recognizes that some people may shrug their shoulders arguing that what matters is not how the pie is divided but the size of the pie.

Stiglitz, however, argues that this argument is fundamentally wrong for four weak reasons, which he seems to believe are strong. First, he says, growing inequality is the flip side of something else: shrinking opportunity. Second, many of the distortions that lead to inequality—such as those associated with monopoly power and preferential tax treatment for special interests—undermine the efficiency of the economy. Third, inequality blocks the "collective actions" that are needed in a modern economy—meaning investment in infrastructure, education and technology. Fourth, because of the increased concentration of income, the majority of the population will not be able to afford an education, and this will lead to their further impoverishment, which in turn will make it harder to get educated, until, one can assume, the United States would fall into general misery.

After Stiglitz published his thoughts, the discussion of the growing inequality has tended to become a moralistic one, in which those saying that it is bad have taken the high moral ground. They portray any doubt about Stiglitz's arguments as a defense of the people who are now in the famous 1%—many of which, like the members of other social strata, are not beyond criticism regarding the way they acquired their wealth. But, as I argue later, that is not the issue. The points are whether inequality is bad in itself, and whether Stiglitz has proven that it is. He has not, as a cursory review of his arguments demonstrates.

In the first place, growing inequality is most frequently the flip side of growing, not shrinking opportunity. In fact, inequality is the mechanism through which the market generates and spreads

Wealth, when invested in new construction, development of communities, infrastructure improvements, and new businesses, can benefit even those people with lower incomes.

innovation, which in turn generates opportunities for millions of individuals. Every innovation has initially generated inequality in incomes, as their inventors exploit it commercially. The inequality, in turn, attracts new innovators, as well as imitators, rapidly spreading the initial innovation and improvements on it. In the process, they generate many new opportunities.

For example, Steve Jobs and Thomas Alva Edison actually created new inventions and enterprises for the sake of putting themselves on the best side of inequality—to make large amounts of money that would increase their income over that of the rest of the population. By being successful, they created inequality not just in their immediate neighborhood but also in the whole country. They became billionaires. Many of their colleagues in Apple and all the Edison companies (General Electric, Consolidated Edison, Commonwealth Edison) also became billionaires in the midst of a society in which just a few people are billionaires. By improving the productivity of others, however, their innovations created millions of new opportunities across nations and continents. Even people who suffer when seeing that others get rich have to recognize that seeing Jobs and

Edison becoming billionaires was a small price to pay for the enormous opportunities they created in the whole world.

Stiglitz's second argument, that many of the distortions that lead to inequality, such as monopoly power and tax privileges undermine the efficiency of the economy, is absolutely irrelevant for the discussion of inequality. It refers to bad practices that are bad independently from their impact on inequality. Certainly, some people may have arrived into the one percent group by objectionable means—like many financiers that became billionaires while bankrupting their firms and their customers, or by obtaining rents from the government. This, however, cannot be constructed into a condemnation of inequality. In fact, fiscal measures that Stiglitz himself would seem to support—like taking away income from the productive to transfer it to the nonproductive—are as negative in terms of the efficiency of the economy as the abuse of monopoly power. Some of these transfers are justifiable only in humanitarian, not economic, grounds. Some other transfers, like subsidies to the rich funded with general taxes, are not justifiable, period. Could we say that equality is bad because some of the means to attain it undermine the efficiency of the economy?

Stiglitz's third argument is not only twisted but also as irrelevant as the second. His efforts to connect the lack of investment in infrastructure, education and technology with income inequality are far fetched to say the least. There are no reliable data on the distribution of income during the crucial 1870 to 1914 period that witnessed the industrialization of the United States. However, it is undeniable that the economic and political influence of the great barons of the epoch (J. P. Morgan, Andrew Carnegie, John D. Rockefeller, Cornelius Vanderbilt Andrew Mellon and Leland Stanford, to mention a few) was unparalleled in the history of the country. And they not only spearheaded the construction of the infrastructure of the country. They also presided over the improvement of education and health that propelled the United States to become the leading power in the world. In fact, these people funded the great expansion of the modern private universities and hospitals in the country. They were the 1% of those years. The current one percent keeps on funding these institutions. Why should they do in private (support hospitals and universities) what Stiglitz say they oppose doing as a class?

Rather than being a result of the concentration of wealth and income, the decline of investment in education and physical infrastructure seems to be attributable to the growing entitlements that plague the federal budget, which are, in turn, the result of a misguided search for equality.

Regarding the fourth argument, the sinking hole of inequality leading to less education and more inequality, it is important to note that the United States has never produced as many graduates as it does today. According to the Economist's 2010 piece, "The Disposable Academic," the annual production of PhDs in the United States doubled to 64,000 from 1970 to today. Moreover, the United States continues to be one of the major sources of knowledge and learning in the entire world. No country in the world has contributed what just Palo Alto has contributed to the current technological revolution, much less what California and the country as a whole have done. According to a recent article in the *Spectator*, philanthropy aimed at helping students is booming in the United States. Twenty-two out of the 30 best universities in the world are American.

Many people from China, India and other developing countries, visibly poorer than the average American student, come to the United States to study. Should we believe that American families, who have access to universities of all prices and generous student loans, cannot afford what the poor Chinese and Indians can, only because the distribution of income of two of the poorest countries in the world is less unequal by a tad than that of the United States? Believing that the United States will enter a vicious circle of lack of education and lower opportunity leading to less education and more poverty is, to say the least, melodramatic.

Thus, Stiglitz's arguments do not resist the slightest confrontation with reality. Unforgivingly for an economist, he seems to ignore the role that inequality plays in generating innovation and growth and, through these, in eliminating poverty.

Actually, Stiglitz does not seem to realize three important points. First, that the real problem is not inequality but poverty. Nobody would say that there is a serious social problem in a city block where Marissa Ann Mayer (the president of Yahoo, who earned $36.6 million in the first six months in her position) lives side by side with a person who earns $200,000 per year, just because Mayer's salary is 366 times that of her neighbor. However, a serious social problem would exist in another block where one neighbor earning $200,000 per year has a salary 366 times that of his neighbor. In that case, the other neighbor would be earning $546 per year. He would be destitute. The problem is not

the inequality, which is the same in both cases, but the poverty of this other neighbor.

Second, Stiglitz does not seem to realize that in many cases inequality could be the price of the reduction of poverty through the mechanism we already discussed—the creation of opportunities. In 1981, China was equalitarian in income terms but also very poor. There were no incentives to improve because everybody earned the same. As the Chinese economy was liberalized, opportunities arose for many potential entrepreneurs to generate new economic activities, hire people and become rich. As they succeeded in their undertakings, inequality rose. But poverty declined, because, as they became millionaires, they created new and better employment, and new and better opportunities for other entrepreneurs.

In fact, one could ask Stiglitz, if there is no potential for inequality, what would be the incentive for innovations and growth?

A third point that Stiglitz seems to ignore is that, if he were right regarding the sinking hole of education and inequality, development would be impossible, because people in the poor countries (like, say, Sweden and Japan were in the nineteenth century or China and Korea and Singapore in the twentieth) would asphyxiate in their own poverty without affording an education. In fact, internationally there is no relationship between inequality and growth. According to Stiglitz, countries with larger inequality should not grow, especially because many of them are poor and would be trapped even more in the sinking hole. But this is not true. Some unequal countries grew faster than some less unequal, and vice versa. No clothes in this emperor.

More than a decade ago I noted the trend to income concentration and predicted that it would continue for many years in a book called *The Triumph of the Flexible Society: The Connectivity Revolution and Resistance to Change* (Praeger, 2003). I did it in the context of the strains introduced by the emergence of the knowledge society within the structures of industrial and agrarian societies. Those who are taking an advantage of this transformation are earning enormous rents. To gain from it you don't have to be a knowledge entrepreneur but only to live in the neighborhood of one of them. California and the entire United States have benefited from Silicon Valley—even the local supermarkets. With time, this trend to concentration of income will reverse itself, as more people learn to take advantage of the economic revolution.

That is, inequality is the mechanism that will spread the benefits of the new knowledge society across the entire world. Without it, there would be no incentive to spread it, and the world would lose the most exciting opportunity to increase its wealth and reduce its poverty since the emergence of the Industrial Revolution. I repeat that this does not mean that I defend the people who have become part of the 1% by state intervention and other bad practices. That is another subject entirely.

EVALUATING THE AUTHOR'S ARGUMENTS:

In this viewpoint, author Manuel Hinds argues that the problem is poverty, not inequality. Do you agree? The author further argues that "inequality could be the price of the reduction of poverty." Does it make sense to fight poverty, inequality, or both? Why?

Income Is a Reward for Labor

Anne Bradley

"Income is a return for labor that is well-invested, because well-invested labor creates value for others."

In the following viewpoint, Anne Bradley debates inequality from the perspective of her Christian faith. The author argues that income should be a reward for labor. If someone provides a valuable service and gets a high income, everyone benefits from the goods or services created. Anne Bradley is an economist and professor of economics. The Institute for Faith, Work & Economics is a Christian organization "advancing a free and flourishing society by revolutionizing the way people view their work."

AS YOU READ, CONSIDER THE FOLLOWING QUESTIONS:

1. What does the author mean by "well-invested labor creates value for others"?
2. Why does the author claim that giving everyone an equal amount of money won't increase income equality?
3. Is a Christian perspective integral to this viewpoint, or does the religious view make no difference?

When someone gets ahead of others financially because of hard work, calculated risk-taking, and innovation, it is not only good—it should be celebrated.

"Is There Such Thing as "Good" Income Inequality?" by Anne Bradley, Institute for Faith, Work & Economics, April 3, 2018. Reprinted by permission.

Bill Gates is worth $110 billion, making him one of the world's richest people. Does the entrepreneur's immense wealth take away opportunity from the rest of us?

Really? Shouldn't Christians be more focused on equality? What about helping the little guy?

Let's think about these questions from an economic perspective.

Isn't Inequality a Sign of Injustice?

Income is a return for labor that is well-invested, because well-invested labor creates value for others. This doesn't occur in a vacuum; we can only earn income when we give others what they want at high quality and reasonable prices. Income is an important incentive for innovation and making goods and services cheaper.

Only when the poor in the third world can earn higher wages, retain their income, and enter the global marketplace will they be on the road out of poverty.

In the United States, we argue against income inequality primarily based on the false idea that if someone earns a high income, they take away opportunities for the poor and middle classes to earn more, too. The truth is, when economies are based on market trade they are not zero-sum games. If one earns a high income because they provide a valuable service, then everyone is better-off because we benefit from a good or service in which we would not have otherwise been provided. Furthermore, value can increasingly be created as people use resources and trade in ways that satisfy their preferences and needs.

When someone earns more, it is because they have created new value for others. Neurosurgery is a highly specialized and highly valuable skill, and the market rewards it accordingly. Because a neurosurgeon has a set of highly sought-after skills that most don't have, he or she earns an income that reflects that. Income is the price of one's labor and, like all other prices, it reflects the supply of the skills required to do the work against the consumers' demand for those skills.

Capitalism will ultimately pull the third world into the first world and give the approximately 620 million people worldwide who are living in extreme poverty the washing machines, antibiotics, and food they so desperately need.

Why Forced Equality Doesn't Work

Though often well-intentioned, any attempt to correct or fix income inequality will fall flat, because egalitarianism (making everyone have the same) is antithetical to our God-given design.

Imagine that in an effort to attain income equality, we were all given an equal amount of money by the government. Let's make this hypothetical income $50,000. For a family of four in the United States living at or below the poverty standard, this would at least double their income. If this happens on day one, what does day two look like? How about a week or a month or a year later? There is no way to ensure that people's amount of cash (based on the amount they were initially given) would remain equal, because we would all do something different with our money based on our unique preferences, needs, choices, and situations.

- Some would put money in a high-risk investment and triple their money.
- Some would invest in a high-risk venture and lose it all.
- Some would put funds in a safe and low-interest money market account and earn a return at a lower rate.
- Some would waste it all at the blackjack table.

There is no way to ensure that income equality is retained unless we constantly redistribute excess earnings (anything greater than $50,000).

The good news is that in a healthy, market-based economy, we have the best chance we have ever had in human history for both high incomes and wealth.

For example, Bill Gates's dramatically high income does not hurt the ability of the janitor to earn an income. The difference in their two incomes has to do with supply and demand for the skills each provides.

The difference in their incomes also has nothing to do with their worth or dignity. God does not define us by our incomes, but he does understand our hearts. If we covet money and make it an idol, it doesn't matter whether we are poor or rich—our hearts need transformation. As such, it is neither inherently righteous to be poor any more than it is villainous to be rich.

Understanding how market economies operate in light of biblical teachings about work and income helps us to better understand these principles. As Christians, we can view this type of "good" income inequality as desirable so long as it is within the context of market trade, private property rights, a sound rule of law, and value creation.

EVALUATING THE AUTHOR'S ARGUMENTS:

In this viewpoint, author Anne Bradley argues that an individual's income is tied to the value they create. Do you think this is true? Why or why not? Review Chapter 1, Viewpoints 4 and 5, which discuss income gaps based on race and gender. Can those statistics be reconciled with the idea that people get the incomes they deserve?

Chapter 3

How Can Income Inequality Be Reduced?

If the income gap is indeed a problem, what steps can be taken to reduce it?

Viewpoint 1

Raising the Minimum Wage Helps Everyone

"A hike in the minimum in fact increases wages for other workers, too, including relatively high earners."

Lisa Camner McKay

In the following viewpoint, Lisa Camner McKay addresses the potential effects of raising the minimum wage. Clearly, raising the minimum wage will provide a higher income for those who continue making the minimum wage. Studies by economists suggest that other wages may also go up. Top earners experience the least increase. The minimum wage and wage inequality are inversely correlated. That means when the minimum wage goes up, wage inequality goes down. Meanwhile, raising the minimum wage had very small effects on unemployment and productivity. Lisa Camner McKay is a banking expert and economics writer.

AS YOU READ, CONSIDER THE FOLLOWING QUESTIONS:
1. What did the economists learn from the example of Brazil increasing its minimum wage?
2. How did economists test whether raising the minimum wage was actually responsible for reducing wage inequality?
3. How does competitive pressure play into the issue?

"Reducing Inequality with the Minimum Wage," by Lisa Camner McKay, Federal Reserve Bank of Minneapolis, June 26, 2018. Reprinted by permission.

Debate over raising the minimum wage often focuses on whether jobs will disappear. But economists have become increasingly interested in how an increase to the minimum might affect other outcomes as well, such as output and inequality.

A higher minimum wage will obviously raise pay for those who remain employed at the new minimum. But in a working paper for the Minneapolis Fed's Opportunity & Inclusive Growth Institute, economists Niklas Engbom and Christian Moser find that a hike in the minimum in fact increases wages for other workers, too, including relatively high earners.

The lowest earners enjoy a substantial increase when the minimum wage goes up, the economists find; middle earners receive a moderate increase, and top earners experience little or no rise. The result, therefore, is that "the policy change induced a notable decline in earnings inequality," write Engbom and Moser, in "Earnings Inequality and the Minimum Wage: Evidence from Brazil" (IWP7). "At the same time, employment and output fall only modestly as workers relocate to more productive firms."

Engbom, a Princeton economist, and Institute visiting scholar Moser of Columbia University analyze the consequences of minimum wage changes in Brazil, specifically, to see if its 119 percent increase in inflation-adjusted minimum wage between 1996 and 2012 can explain a substantial decline in wage inequality that occurred over the same time. The data display a remarkable inverse pattern. Did the rise in minimum wage cause the decline in inequality? And if so, how?

Modeling Job Search

That the minimum wage and wage inequality are (inversely) correlated does not prove causality, of course. So Engbom and Moser build a labor market model to determine how the two might be related. The model's workers, searching for jobs, have different skill levels. Firms, which vary in productivity, choose the wage for each job and decide how often to post vacancies. Setting a lower wage will increase the firm's per-worker profit, but a higher wage means finding a worker more quickly. This trade-off leads more productive firms to

Studies in Brazil have shown that raising the minimum wage can help nearly everyone, with the exception of top earners. These wage hikes bring about a decrease in income inequality. Would the results be the same in the United States?

offer higher wages. Thus Engbom and Moser are able to re-create the real-world observation that wages vary across firms even for workers with the same skills.

They then use data from the Brazilian Ministry of Labor and Employment to fit their model to Brazil's labor market by matching features such as the rate at which employed workers find new jobs and the wages that workers are willing to accept.

Next, the researchers simulate the effects of a minimum wage hike like that experienced in Brazil. The result is wage increases for workers from the 1st through the 80th percentile of the earnings distribution. The increase is largest for low-skill workers and gradually declines for higher-earnings groups. The result: The gap between top and bottom earners shrinks, thereby reducing earnings inequality.

Why does this happen? When low-productivity firms increase their wages to meet the new minimum, high-productivity firms increase wages, too, because they want to attract workers quickly. They need to outbid low-productivity firms with better offers than they made before the wage hike.

"Such competitive pressure leads the minimum wage to spill over to higher-paying firms," Engbom and Moser write. Firms are able to offer higher wages because the labor market was not fully competitive to begin with: Workers were being paid less than their marginal product, with firms capturing the extra profit.

Big Change to Inequality, Small Change to Employment

Engbom and Moser also use their model to evaluate other macroeconomic consequences of an increase in the minimum wage. Notably, nonemployment (in Brazil, this includes unemployment and informal employment) increases by 0.4 percentage points, while gross output declines by a modest 0.1 percent. These macroeconomic effects are muted, the economists explain, because in a labor market that is not fully competitive, the minimum wage increase leads to "efficient reallocation of workers toward more productive firms." In other words, increasing the Brazilian minimum wage actually led to small efficiency gains as well as a large reduction in earnings inequality.

One takeaway is that a policy that nominally affects only a small share of workers—those who were making less than the new minimum wage—in fact influences wages for most workers. Engbom and Moser suggest that future research might examine whether other labor market policies that in theory affect just a subset of the labor force (such as unemployment benefits and antidiscrimination laws) also have more far-reaching impact. It would also be interesting to extend the model to the United States, where recent significant increases to the minimum wage have been enacted or proposed at the local level in a number of major cities, including San Francisco, Chicago, New York and Minneapolis.

EVALUATING THE AUTHOR'S ARGUMENTS:

In this viewpoint, Lisa Camner McKay argues that increasing the minimum wage will do more good than harm to the economy. Do you agree with her conclusions? How confident can we be that the example from Brazil will work in the United States? How else might we test these theories?

Address Segregation to End the Income Gap

Joe Cortright

"There are good reasons to believe that high levels of segregation impair the relative economic opportunities available to black Americans."

In the following viewpoint, Joe Cortright discusses how race plays into income inequality. Where communities are largely separated by race, income inequality is much higher. In communities with more segregation, poorer neighborhoods typically house people of color. They may have less access to good schools, public services, and social networks that could provide job leads. In addition, having a low income may tend to keep people in the poorer neighborhood. While we can't yet be certain how cause and effect are related, it seems likely that reducing racial segregation would reduce the income gap. Joe Cortright is president and principal economist of Impresa, a consulting firm specializing in regional economic analysis. City Observatory is a think tank devoted to data-driven analysis of cities.

AS YOU READ, CONSIDER THE FOLLOWING QUESTIONS:
1. How much of a difference does racial segregation make when it comes to the income gap between blacks and whites?
2. What negative effects for black neighborhoods can come from racial segregation?
3. How confident can we be that the studies prove the cause of the racial income gap?

Income inequality in the United States has a profoundly racial dimension. As income inequality has increased, one feature of inequality has remained very much unchanged: black incomes remain persistently lower than white incomes. But while that pattern holds for the nation as a whole, it's interesting to note that in some places the black/white income gap is much smaller. One characteristic of these more equal places is a lower level of racial segregation.

Nationally, the average black household has an income 42 percent lower than average white household. But that figure masks huge differences from one metropolitan area to another. And though any number of factors may influence the size of a place's racial income gap, just one of them—residential segregation—allows you to predict as much as 60 percent of all variation in the income gap from city to city. Although income gaps between whites and blacks are large and persistent across the country, they are much smaller in more integrated metropolitan areas and larger in more segregated metropolitan areas. The strength of this relationship strongly suggests that reducing the income gap will necessarily require reducing racial segregation.

To get a picture of this relationship, we've assembled data on segregation and the black/white earnings gap for the largest U.S. metropolitan areas. [Plotted on a chart it] shows the relationship between the black/white earnings disparity (on the vertical axis), and the degree of black/white segregation (on the horizontal axis). Here, segregation is measured with something called the dissimilarity index, which essentially measures what percent of each group would have to move to create a completely integrated region. (Higher numbers therefore indicate more segregated places.) To measure the black-white income

The income gap between black and white Americans appears to be lower in neighborhoods that are racially integrated.

gap, we first calculated per capita black income as a percentage of per capita white income, and then took the difference from 100. (A metropolitan area where black income was 100% of white income would have no racial income gap, and would receive a score of zero; a metro area where black income was 90% of white income would receive a score of 10.)

The positive slope to the line indicates that as segregation increases, the gap between black income and white incomes grows as black incomes fall relative to white incomes. On average, each five-percentage-point decline in the dissimilarity index is associated with an three-percentage-point decline in the racial income gap (The r2 for this relationship is .59, suggesting a close relationship between relative income and segregation).

What's less clear is which way the causality goes, or in what proportions. That is to say: there are good reasons to believe that high levels of segregation impair the relative economic opportunities available to black Americans. Segregation may have the effect of limiting an individual's social networks, lowering the quality of public services, decreasing access to good schools, and increasing risk of exposure to crime, all of which may limit or reduce economic success. This is especially true in neighborhoods of concentrated poverty, which tend to be disproportionately neighborhoods of color.

But there are also good reasons to believe that in places where black residents have relatively fewer economic opportunities, they will end up more segregated than in places where there are more opportunities. Relatively less income means less buying power when it comes to real estate, and less access to the wealthier neighborhoods that, in a metropolitan area with a large racial income gap, will be disproportionately white. A large difference between white and black earnings may also suggest related problems—like a particularly hostile white population—that would also lead to more segregation.

The data shown here is consistent with earlier and more recent research of the negative effects of segregation. Glaeser and Cutler found that higher levels of segregation were correlated with worse economic outcomes for blacks. Likewise, racial and income segregation was one of several factors that Raj Chetty and his colleagues found were strongly correlated with lower levels of inter-generational economic mobility at the metropolitan level.

Implications

To get a sense of how this relationship plays out in particular places, consider the difference between two Southern metropolitan areas: Birmingham and Raleigh. Birmingham is more segregated (dissimilarity 65) than Raleigh (dissimilarity 41). The black white income gap is significantly smaller in Raleigh (blacks earn 17 percent less than whites) than it is in Birmingham (blacks earn 29 percent less than whites).

The size and strength of this relationship point up the high stakes in continuing to make progress in reducing segregation as a means of reducing the racial income gap. If Detroit had the same levels of segregation as the typical large metro (with a dissimilarity index of 60, instead of 80), you would expect its racial gap to be 12 percentage points smaller, which translates to $3,000 more in annual income for the average black resident.

These data presented here and the other research cited are a strong reminder that if we're going to address the persistent racial gap in income, we'll most likely need to make further progress in reducing racial segregation in the nation's cities.

The correlations shown here don't dispose of the question of causality: this cross sectional evidence doesn't prove that segregation causes a higher black-white income gap. It is entirely possible that the reverse is true: that places with smaller income gaps between blacks and whites have less segregation, in part because higher relative incomes for blacks afford them greater choices in metropolitan housing markets. It may be the case that causation runs in both directions. In the US, there are few examples of places that stay segregated that manage to close the income gap; there are few places that have closed the income gap that have not experienced dramatically lower levels of segregation. Increased racial integration appears to be at least a corollary, if not a cause of reduced levels of income disparity between blacks and whites in US metropolitan areas.

If we're concerned about the impacts of gentrification on the well-being of the nation's African American population, we should recognize that anything that promotes greater racial integration in metropolitan areas is likely to be associated with a reduction in the black-white income gap; and conversely, maintaining segregation is likely to be an obstacle to diminishing this gap.

Though provocative, these data don't control for a host of other factors that we know are likely to influence the economic outcomes of individuals, including the local industrial base and educational attainment. It would be helpful to have a regression analysis that estimated the relationship between the black white earnings gap and education. It may be the case that the smaller racial income gap in less segregated cities may be attributable to higher rates of black educational attainment in those cities. For example, the industry mix in

Raleigh may have lower levels of racial pay disparities and employment patterns than the mix of industries in Birmingham. But even the industry mix may be influenced by the segregation pattern of cities; firms that have more equitable practices may gravitate towards, or grow more rapidly in communities with lower levels of segregation.

Brief Background on Racial Income Gaps and Segregation

Two enduring hallmarks of race in America are racial segregation and a persistent gap between the incomes of whites and blacks. In 2011, median household income for White, Non-Hispanic Households was $55,412; for Blacks $32,366 (Census Bureau, Income, Poverty, and Health Insurance Coverage in the United States: 2011, Table A-1). For households, the racial income gap between blacks and whites is 42 percent. Census Bureau data shows on average, black men have per capita incomes that are about 64 percent that of Non-Hispanic White men. This gap has narrowed only slightly over the past four decades: in the early 1980s the income of black men was about 59 percent that of Non-Hispanic whites.

Because the advantage of whites' higher annual incomes compounds over time, racial wealth disparities are even greater than disparities in earnings. Lifetime earnings for African-Americans are about 25 percent less than for similarly aged Non-Hispanic White Americans. The Urban Institute estimated that the net present value of lifetime earnings for a non-hispanic white person born in late 1940s would be about $2 million compared to just $1.5 million for an African-American born the same year.

In the past half century, segregation has declined significantly. Nationally, the black/non-black dissimilarity index has fallen from an all-time high of 80 in 1970 to 55 in 2010, according to Glaeser and Vigdor. The number of all-white census tracts has declined from one in five to one in 427. Since 1960, the share of African-Americans living in majority-non-black areas increased from less than 30 percent to almost 60 percent. Still, there are wide variations among metropolitan areas, many of which remain highly segregated.

Technical Notes

We measure the racial income gap by comparing the per capita income of blacks in each metropolitan area with the per capita income of whites in that same metropolitan area. These data are from Brown University's US 2010 project, and have been compiled from the 2005-09 American Community Survey. The Brown researchers compiled this data separately for the metropolitan divisions that make up several large metropolitan areas (New York, Chicago, Miami, Philadelphia, San Francisco, Seattle, Dallas and others). For these tabulations we report the segregation and racial income gaps reported for the most populous metropolitan division in each metropolitan area.

EVALUATING THE AUTHOR'S ARGUMENTS:

In this viewpoint, author Joe Cortright suggests that ending racial segregation would help reduce the income gap. Should communities institute policies to reduce segregation, with the goal of reducing income inequality? If so, what might these policies look like?

Tax Rates Haven't Addressed Income Inequality— Yet

"Taxes have not exacerbated increasing income inequality but have not done much to offset it."

Frank Sammartino

In the following viewpoint, Frank Sammartino discusses how the US government's tax policies have affected income inequality. He notes income inequality has increased in the United States and around the world. In the United States, taxes have become more progressive. This means people with higher incomes pay a higher percentage of their income in taxes. This should reduce inequality. However, taxes have also lowered overall. This reduces the effect of progressive taxes on income inequality. In short, the author argues, taxes have not offset income inequality. Frank Sammartino is an economist who has worked at the Congressional Budget Office.

"Taxes and Income Inequality," by Frank Sammartino, Urban-Brookings Tax Policy Center, June 15, 2017. Reprinted by permission.

This year, Congress will consider what may be the biggest tax bill in decades. This is one of a series of briefs the Tax Policy Center has prepared to help people follow the debate. Each focuses on a key tax policy issue that Congress and the Trump administration may address.

Income inequality has increased sharply over the past 35 years. What role has the federal tax system played in creating—or reducing—inequality?

Increasing Income Inequality

A simple way to measure inequality is by looking at the share of income received by the highest-income people. Using a broad measure that includes labor, business, and capital income; government cash payments (such as Social Security); and the value of in-kind benefits from government programs (such as Medicare and Medicaid), the Congressional Budget Office finds that the income share of the top fifth of the population rose from 43 to 53 percent between 1979 and 2013. This increase in income inequality came about despite the growth in Social Security, Medicare, and Medicaid, which provide the greatest boost in before-tax income to low- and middle-income households.

Much of the gain in the top income share went to the top 1 percent of the population. In 1979, they received 9 percent of all income. By 2013, their share grew to 15 percent, more than all the income received by the bottom 40 percent. The income measure includes realized capital gains, which are sensitive to business cycle fluctuations and to changes in tax rates. Because realized capital gains are a significant income component for the top 1 percent, their income share is more volatile than income shares of other groups.

Top income shares have not reached these levels since the 1920s. After falling precipitously during the Great Depression and World War II, the income share of the top 1 percent leveled off during the next three decades. It began climbing again in the 1980s, interrupted only by the 2001 and 2008–09 recessions. Since the stock market rebound, income shares of the top 1 percent have increased again.

A Worldwide Phenomenon

The United States is not the only country with increasing income inequality. Most member countries of the Organisation for Economic Co-operation and Development have experienced the same phenomenon, though to a lesser degree than the United States.

The Role of Taxes

The figures so far only consider income before taxes. What happens after we account for taxes?

The US federal tax system is progressive. High-income households pay a larger share of their income in total federal taxes than low-income households. State and local taxes, which are not included in this analysis, are much less progressive, and some, such as sales taxes, are regressive (low-income households pay a higher share of their income in sales taxes than high-income households).

Because federal taxes are progressive, the distribution of after-tax income is more equal than income before taxes. High-income households have a slightly smaller share of total income after taxes than their share of income before taxes, while the reverse is true for other income groups.

Federal taxes are more progressive than they were 35 years ago. Although the average tax rate for high-income households has varied a lot, the average tax rate for these households was nearly the same in recent years as at its peaks in 1977 and 1995. Meanwhile, the average tax rate for middle- and low-income groups dropped incrementally from the early 1980s through 2007 and then fell dramatically from 2007 through 2009 because of temporary tax cuts enacted in

Federal income taxes have changed over the years, but these changes have not affected income inequality significantly.

response to the Great Recession. Average rates rebounded as those tax cuts expired, but by 2013, remained well below their 1979 values for those groups.

Effect of Taxes on Income Inequality

A more progressive tax system would reduce income inequality if nothing else changes. But while federal taxes became more progressive, they also were shrinking relative to before-tax income starting in 2001, thanks to tax cuts during the administrations of George W. Bush and Barack Obama. A lower average tax rate offset the equalizing effect of increased tax progressivity, leaving the effect of federal taxes on income inequality little changed.

A widely used measure of income inequality is the Gini index. The index has a value of zero when income is distributed equally across all income groups and a value of one when the highest income group receives all the income. By this measure, inequality has been consistently lower for after-tax income than for before-tax income.

The gap between the index for before-tax and after-tax incomes measures how much taxes reduce inequality. The bigger the difference, the more taxes equalize income. The gap closed during the 1980s as taxes relative to income fell more for high-income households than for low-income groups. But as federal taxes became more progressive starting in the 1980s, the gap between before-tax and after-tax income inequality widened. It remains at roughly the pre-1980 level.

The bottom line is that before-tax income inequality has risen since the 1970s, despite an increase in government transfer payments. Because high-income people pay higher average tax rates than others, federal taxes reduce inequality. But the mitigating effect of taxes is about the same today as before 1980. Thus, after-tax income inequality has increased about as much as before-tax inequality. Taxes have not exacerbated increasing income inequality, but have not done much to offset it.

EVALUATING THE AUTHOR'S ARGUMENTS:

In this viewpoint, author Frank Sammartino says taxes have not yet addressed income inequality. What can you conclude from this? Should tax rates be changed? Why or why not, and if so, how?

Reducing Income Inequality Hurts the Poor

"Income inequality has resulted from things few people would want to 'correct'— namely, individual freedom and the success of markets in satisfying the masses."

Dwight R. Lee

In the following viewpoint, Dwight R. Lee argues that the inclination to transfer wealth or increase government entitlement programs in order to reduce income inequality is counterproductive. The author notes that government transfer programs are ineffective. What helps reduce poverty, he claims, is economic freedom. Even though market economies might result in income inequality, they also increase growth and opportunities for the poor. Not everyone will be as rich as innovators like Bill Gates and Oprah Winfrey, but we are all better off for the system that created them. Dwight R. Lee is the O'Neil Professor of Global Markets and Freedom in the Cox School of Business at Southern Methodist University.

AS YOU READ, CONSIDER THE FOLLOWING QUESTIONS:
1. Why is it better to "be poor in Cleveland than in Calcutta," according to the author?
2. How does the author use the reduction in arranged marriages to help make his argument?
3. How do government transfer programs often perpetuate poverty, according to the viewpoint?

Market economies motivate positive-sum activities in which people become rich by creating more wealth for others—both in the form of higher-paying jobs and improved goods and services at lower prices. That doesn't mean everyone will earn the same, but it means improved conditions for everyone, even the least well off. It is far better, after all, to be poor in Cleveland than in Calcutta.

Yet when people talk about increasing income inequality, they almost always discuss the topic as a market failure calling for government correction. They invariably ignore the possibility that increased income inequality has resulted from things few people would want to "correct"—namely, individual freedom and the success of markets in satisfying the needs and wants of the masses.

Four such successes come to mind.

To begin with, the returns on education have increased significantly in recent years, as reflected in the increased salaries and wages that come with more education. This increased return is exactly what we should want as technological progress increases the productivity of those who acquire more knowledge and improve their abstract reasoning skills relative to those who do not.

Second, profound social, economic, and political changes have combined to remove barriers to market access by women. Half the population now has full participation in a marketplace that had for generations been closed to them. More women than ever are taking advantage of the market's opportunities, often building on advanced degrees. Among those women, more are now majoring in fields that yield the highest returns. This choice goes a long way toward explaining why income inequality between men and women in the

Higher education, even considering its high cost, pays off when it comes to increased salaries and wages. Correcting income inequality could change that. The viewpoint author suggests several "successes" that result from an income gap.

United States has declined in recent decades. In many fields—once factors such as differences in major, career selection, and duration of employment are controlled for—income disparities between the sexes evaporate. Despite this relatively equality between the genders, we should expect to find increasing income inequality among women as more women ascend to high-salary positions.

Third, the day has long passed in most countries when marriages were arranged without the consent of the betrothed. This freedom, along with the increased mobility people enjoy in wealthy countries, means that marriage markets in those countries are highly competitive, with each participant putting his or her looks, personalities, and prospects on offer to compete for someone who best satisfies what he or she is looking for in a partner. With more women getting advanced degrees and working alongside high-earning colleagues, marriage markets have generated more matches between individuals who each have high earning potential.

Fourth, spurts of technological progress create big winners. But the resulting technological improvements leave everyone better off by making possible what has always been required for sustainable improvements in our general living standards: the production of more value with less effort and fewer resources—all while increasing the economically relevant resource base.

For example, technological progress has recently made it possible for almost everyone in wealthy countries to enjoy the performances of the very best athletes, musicians, singers, talk-show hosts, comedians, etc., wherever they are, with visual and audio clarity that rivals and often exceeds that of live performances. Between those who entertain and those who bring the entertainment to our eyes at relatively low cost, we are bound to find high earners. In other words, technological access explains why people such as Tiger Woods, Britney Spears, and Oprah Winfrey have earned incomes that comparably skilled athletes and entertainers could not have imagined a few decades ago. Those entrepreneurs who develop ways to provide the most value to consumers at the lowest costs, such as Bill Gates, Mark Zuckerberg, Michael Dell, and Jeff Bezos, also become billionaires at young ages. These achievements are consistent with other periods of rapid technological progress. One ambitious and intelligent individual, willing to take a big risk, can come up with the sorts of products and services that improve the lives of millions by offering them low-cost opportunities to be entertained, enlightened, and connected.

It is difficult to imagine how anyone interested in improving the welfare of the least advantaged would want to lessen income inequality by reversing any of the four socioeconomic trends above. The increased prosperity these trends have made possible for the most successful among us is obvious. The increased prosperity and well-being for the poor is no less real, but these gains are commonly ignored in discussions of income inequality.

Although creating more wealth is the most effective way of reducing poverty—and happens also to be a great way to become fabulously wealthy—one standard argument is that the poor would be better off if government reduced income inequality simply by transferring more money from the rich to the poor.

The serious problem with this argument is that government transfers have never been very effective at reducing income inequality or improving the conditions of the poor. Ironically, most government transfers go to those who are not poor. The two largest federal transfer programs, Social Security and Medicare, are targeted to the elderly, most of whom are not poor (medical care for the poor is provided by Medicaid). Many seniors are poorer than they would otherwise be, though, because these programs reduce the incentives for people to save for their old

age. These two transfer programs make up close to one-third of all federal spending, and there are many billions of other federal transfer dollars going to politically influential recipients who are not poor and are often quite wealthy (e.g., large agribusiness concerns, defense contractors, pharmaceutical giants, etc).

Of course, some government transfer dollars and in-kind benefits do go to the poor, but they often perpetuate poverty among the most economically disadvantaged. When the poor make an effort to improve their skills and work hard to increase their incomes, the government money and benefits they receive are reduced by a large percentage of their additional earnings. Sometimes it's more than 100 percent, leaving them with less take-home income than before. The result is that many poor people see little benefit in making the effort to earn more income, or any income at all. They are trapped in poverty by the very programs that were supposed to help them escape it. (We'll pass over the army of administrators who skim a percentage of these transfers and enjoy lavish benefits.)

Relative economic freedom, despite the income inequality that results, has done far more to help the poor than government transfer programs have ever done. Indeed, government attempts to reduce income inequality would do little to reduce inequality but a great deal to hamper economic growth and reduce economic opportunities for the poor to improve their lives with productive effort.

EVALUATING THE AUTHOR'S ARGUMENTS:

In this viewpoint, author Dwight R. Lee argues that income inequality is not the societal scourge that many purport it to be. Are the specific examples of market freedom the author provides effective in making his case? Do you agree that such freedom improves the lives of everyone in a society, even those at the low end of the economic spectrum? Why or why not?

Paid Family Leave Helps Everyone

"One of the biggest negative beliefs about paid family leave— that it is a burden on business— may not be true."

Jill Cornfield

In the following viewpoint, Jill Cornfield explores how paid family leave affects families and businesses. The government Family and Medical Leave Act (FMLA) provides guidelines for when and how companies must provide their employees with time off. This time off is taken without pay. Receiving family leave with pay would clearly benefit employees. However, many people assume this is not done because it would hurt the employer. The author addresses those concerns and claims that many of them are unfounded. Jill Cornfield writes about personal finance for CNBC.

AS YOU READ, CONSIDER THE FOLLOWING QUESTIONS:
1. What benefits does the Family and Medical Leave Act provide to families? How would this change with paid family leave, according to the author?
2. Is paid leave a burden on businesses, according to the viewpoint?
3. What do the examples of California and New Jersey, which have paid family leave laws, show us?

"Five myths about the burden of family leave on business," by Jill Cornfield, CNBC LLC., September 27, 2018. Reprinted by permission.

The conversation is getting louder. Traditionally, American families have had to go it alone with a new baby. However, paid family leave is starting to gain traction in the U.S. due to employee demand.

And one of the biggest negative beliefs about paid family leave—that it is a burden on business—may not be true.

It's one of the most common arguments against widespread adoption in the U.S.

Under the Family and Medical Leave Act, about 20 million leaves are taken each year—and one-fifth of those are used by families with a new child, according to the Society for Human Resource Management.

The Family and Medical Leave Act allows new parents to take up to 12 weeks off from a job, but it guarantees only that they'll have a job to return to. The act doesn't mandate any salary during that time.

More than half of people surveyed said an unpaid leave for family or medical reasons would mean serious financial hardship, according to a September survey by the National Partnership for Women and Families.

It's a critical issue that isn't going anywhere.

Even before the Family and Medical Leave Act was enacted, small-business owners "often allowed employees time off without the government telling them how to do it," said Molly Day, vice president of public affairs at the National Small Business Association.

Most of the association's members—83 percent—already have some kind of paid sick leave, according to Day, with the majority offering 11 days or more.

The administration of the existing law has been a problem for businesses. "Paperwork and legal requirements have overwhelmed small-business owners," Day said.

It's not that business owners are indifferent to the needs of their workforce. "As small-business owners, our members often employ family members, neighbors and friends," Day said. "They understand the value of providing those employees paid time off."

The problem is the increased paperwork and reporting requirements that crop up in the wake of government involvement regarding "something they're already doing," Day said.

Employees might benefit from the Family and Medical Leave Act after the birth of a child. However, the act does not guarantee the employee will receive a salary during their leave.

On one hand, businesses are concerned about the potential administrative burden, with employees missing weeks at a time and the need to 'on-board' replacements for short periods of time.

On the other hand, some employers favor paid leave because it boosts retention. In the long run, this saves on the expense of employee training.

Common assumptions about the impact on business are increased costs and the administrative burden. These are mostly baseless fears, according to the New York State Paid Family Leave Coalition.

The Benefit Will Be Yet Another Expense

Paid family leave benefits can be fully absorbed by small employee contributions, with zero out-of-pocket contributions by employers to pay for benefits. And because employers aren't paying the wages of the employee on leave, the money can be used, if necessary, to pay any temporary replacement costs or overtime.

Bottom Lines Will Take a Hit

The experiences of employers in states that have similar laws show that paid family leave does not hurt businesses and can even help. In California, most employers reported that paid family leave had a positive or neutral effect on turnover, saving employers the costly step of replacing a staffer.

A majority of California employers also reported positive or neutral effects on productivity (88.5 percent), profitability/performance (91 percent) and employee morale (98.6 percent).

Paid Leave Is a Burden on Small Business

Small businesses that cannot afford the same generous family leave benefits as larger companies are at a competitive disadvantage in hiring. When these smaller companies offer paid family leave through an employee-paid program, it levels the playing field.

Employees Will Abuse Paid Leave

Employees will be required to provide proof of their need for family leave. Studies in California and New Jersey do not reflect abuse in those programs. Data from California and New Jersey show that workers take less than the maximum amount of time allowed by law, supporting the idea that employees take only the time they truly need.

Paid Leave Will Be an Administrative Hassle

Under the New York plan that started earlier this year, for example, there are no substantial new administrative or compliance requirements for employers. Instead, the program builds on the existing disability insurance infrastructure that dates from the 1950s.

Facts About Income Inequality

Editor's note: These facts can be used in reports to add credibility when making important points or claims.

Income is money, or something of equivalent value, received in exchange for work, for goods sold, or through investing capital. Most people receive income from wages (an amount paid per hour of work) or salaries (a fixed amount paid per period). People may also get rent, interest on a savings account, dividends from shares of stock, or profits from selling something for more than they paid for it.

A country's **income inequality** refers to the extent to which income is distributed in an uneven manner among that country's population.

Wealth differs from income. Wealth includes the value of homes, stock, or other possessions.

The **poverty rate** refers to the number of people who have trouble making ends meet. In the U.S., an estimated 140 million people (43.5 percent of the total population) are either poor or low-income. In 2019, a single person was considered to live in poverty if they made less than $12,490 in annual income. For a household of four people, poverty starts at $25,750 per year. For complete poverty rates, see https://aspe.hhs.gov/poverty-guidelines.

People in poverty often have worse health and live shorter lives. Higher rates of income inequality are associated with higher rates of heart problems, infant mortality, and mental illness. Low-income Americans have a dramatically shorter life expectancy than the richest Americans. Men in the top 1 percent of the income distribution live 15 years longer than those in the bottom 1 percent, on average. For women, the difference is about 10 years, on average.

The minimum wage is $7.25 (as of 2019). It has not changed since 2009. The minimum wage pays a full-time worker $15,080 a year. In 2019, the U.S. House of Representatives passed a bill to raise the federal minimum wage to $15 per hour. However, the bill died in the Senate. It was estimated that the bill would have increased the wages of 17 million workers in 2025. It might also have put some people out of work, with estimates on the number ranging from 0 to 3.7 million. Several states and cities already plan to gradually increase the minimum wage to $15 per hour.

The median household income in 2018 was $61,937 (numbers may differ slightly depending on the source). Median income means half of people earn less than that amount and half earn more.

The richest 1 percent of the world's population has 40 percent of its wealth.

The AFL-CIO, a federation of labor unions, reported on executive incomes. In 2018, Chief Executive Officers (CEOs) of 500 large U.S. firms were paid, on average, $14.5 million in total compensation. This is 287 times more than what the median average employee received. In the prior decade, the average S&P 500 CEO's pay increased by $5.2 million. Meanwhile, the average worker's pay increased by $7858.

In general, Americans pay from 10 percent to 37 percent of their income in income taxes. Additional payments go to Social Security and Medicare. By some calculations, the average single American contributes nearly 30 percent of their earnings to income taxes, Medicare, and Social Security. Families pay an average of 24 percent of their income to these taxes. In most states, people also pay sales tax on the goods they buy. Homeowners pay taxes on their property. Some people may get money back from the government, which further changes their tax rate.

What Affects Income

Education increases income. Over a lifetime, Americans with college degrees earn 84% more than those with only high school degrees.

Race affects income. White and Asian workers make over 30 percent more than black and Latinx workers on average. The median family income for African Americans is 56 percent of the median white American family income. Racial discrimination affects education, hiring, and pay practices, which in turn contribute to the earnings gap.

In the 1960s, most white people earned more than the typical black person. That proportion has declined—the racial gap is now smaller. However, overall income inequality has gone up. Reaching the middle of the income distribution no longer provides the same economic rewards.

In 2018, the U.S. median household income was $87,194 for Asian households, $70,642 for Caucasian (white non-Hispanic) homes, $51,450 for Hispanics of any race, and $41,361 for Black households. In most major metropolitan areas, black household income growth outpaced white household income growth. However, median household income was still dramatically higher for whites in every city. While black household income grew at a faster rate, that growth was nowhere near enough to make up for the gap.

Gender affects income. Women make up 63 percent of the workers who earn the federal minimum wage. In addition, women may do far more unpaid work, such as child care. Women tend to hold more college debt and have less retirement savings.

Most of the top earners in the U.S. are men. Women now make up almost half of the country's workforce. Yet among the top 10 percent of earners, only 27 percent are women. Among the top 1 percent of earners, less than 17 percent of workers are women. Women make up only 5 percent of CEOs at Fortune 500 firms. In 2018, the world had 2,208 billionaires. Only 256 of them were women.

Poverty is an especially serious problem for women of color. The national poverty rate for white men is 7.0 percent. Yet poverty affects 21.4 percent of Black women, 18.7 percent of Latinas, and 22.8 percent of Native American women.

According to the National Women's Law Center, households led by single women with children had a poverty rate of 35.6 percent. The rate for households led by single men with children was about half that, 17.3 percent.

Transgender Americans experience poverty at twice the rate of the general population. According to The National Center for Transgender Equality, transgender people of color experience even higher rates of poverty. They found that 43 percent of Latinx, 41 percent of Native American, 40 percent of multiracial, and 38 percent of Black transgender respondents lived in poverty in 2015.

Organizations to Contact

The editors have compiled the following list of organizations concerned with the issues debated in this book. The descriptions are derived from materials provided by the organizations. All have publications or information available for interested readers. The list was compiled on the date of publication of the present volume; the information provided here may change. Be aware that many organizations take several weeks or longer to respond to inquiries, so allow as much time as possible for the receipt of requested materials.

American Federation of Labor and Congress of Industrial Organizations (AFL-CIO)
815 16th Street NW
Washington, DC 20006
contact form: aflcio.org/contact
website: aflcio.org/
The AFL-CIO is a federation of labor unions that works to improve the lives of working people. The website discusses gender equality, global worker rights, and more. See Executive Paywatch at aflcio.org/paywatch for statistics on compensation received by executives versus average workers.

The Fight for $15
email: info@fightfor15.org
website: fightfor15.org/
The Fight for $15 is a union-led movement to increase the US national minimum wage. Learn how the fight is going and why the group encourages underpaid workers to strike.

Institute for Faith, Work & Economics (IFWE)
8227 Old Courthouse Road, Suite 310
Tysons, VA 22182
(703) 962-7877
email: info@tifwe.org

website: tifwe.org

IFWE is a Christian organization that attempts to integrate faith, work, and economics. It posted the article found in Chapter 2, Viewpoint 5. On the website, under the Learn tab, find information on Economics.

Institute for Policy Studies (IPS)

1301 Connecticut Avenue NW, Suite 600
Washington, DC 20036
(202) 234-9382
email: info@ips-dc.org
website: https://ips-dc.org/

IPS is a progressive think tank "dedicated to building a more equitable, ecologically sustainable, and peaceful society." One of its projects is Inequality.org, which tracks inequality-related news and views and provided several of the viewpoints in this book.

National Committee for Pay Equity (NCPE)

email: fairpay@pay-equity.org
website: www.pay-equity.org/

NCPE advocates for pay equity for women and people of color. The website provides research reports on the gender wage gap and how to fight it.

Prosperity Now

1200 G Street NW, Suite 400
Washington, DC 20005
(202) 408-9788
email: hello@prosperitynow.org
website: www.prosperitynow.org/

Prosperity Now is dedicated to helping people prosper, especially people of color and those with low incomes. Learn what programs are available and how to take action.

The Urban-Brookings Tax Policy Center (TPC)
500 L'Enfant Plaza SW
Washington, DC 20024
(202) 833-7200
email: info@taxpolicycenter.org
website: www.taxpolicycenter.org
TPC is made up of experts in tax, budget, and social policy. They provided Viewpoint 3 in Chapter 3. Learn how taxes affect income inequality, study current laws and proposals, and find statistics on income and wealth.

The Washington Center for Equitable Growth
1156 15th Street NW, Suite 700
Washington, DC 20005
(202) 545-6002
contact form: equitablegrowth.org/contact/
website: equitablegrowth.org/
This is a nonprofit organization dedicated to policies that promote strong economic growth. Read the blog, find experts, and learn about the organization's research.

The World Bank Group
1818 H Street NW
Washington, DC 20433 USA
(202) 473-1000
website: www.worldbank.org/
The World Bank Group lists as its goals ending extreme poverty and promoting income growth for the poorest people in every country. The website provides extensive data on poverty along with publications on poverty, economic development, and related topics.

For Further Reading

Books

Banerjee, Abhijit V. And Esther Duflo. *Good Economics for Hard Times*. New York, NY: PublicAffairs, 2019. Nobel Prize winning economists from MIT show how economics can solve social and political problems, including inequality.

Bowles, Samuel. *The Moral Economy: Why Good Incentives Are No Substitute for Good Citizens (Castle Lectures Series).* Yale University press, 2016. Incentives can either help or hurt people and the economy. Historical and recent case studies along with behavioral experiments show how

Eboch, M. M. *Race and Economics (Race in America).* Minneapolis, MN: ABDO Essential Library, 2017. This title explores in detail how race and racism affect economics in America.

Johnston, David Cay. *Divided: The Perils of Our Growing Inequality.* New York, NY: The New Press, 2014. Scholars, activists, and journalists share their views on inequality in America

Lindsey, Brink and Steven Teles. *The Captured Economy*. Oxford, UK: Oxford University Press, 2017. The authors discuss how wealthy special interests capture policymaking for their own benefit.

Piketty, Thomas. *Capital in the Twenty-First Century.* Cambridge, MA: Belknap Press (An Imprint of Harvard University Press), 2014. The author analyzes data from 20 countries to uncover economic and social patterns relating to wealth and inequality.

Posner, Eric A. and E. Glen Weyl. *Radical Markets: Uprooting Capitalism and Democracy for a Just Society.* Princeton, NJ: Princeton University Press, 2019. This book "reveals bold new ways to organize markets for the good of everyone" with open, free, and competitive markets.

Saez, Emmanuel and Gabriel Zucman. *The Triumph of Injustice: How the Rich Dodge Taxes and How to Make Them Pay.* New York, NY: W. W. Norton & Company, 2019. The authors explore America's tax system and conclude that it unfairly helps the wealthy. They suggest a reinvention of taxes.

Sowell, Thomas. *Discrimination and Disparities.* New York, NY: Basic Books; Revised, Enlarged ed. edition, 2019. This book looks at racial disparity in America and challenges the idea that any one factor can determine economic outcomes.

Stiglitz, Joseph E. *The Price of Inequality How Today's Divided Society Endangers Our Future.* New York, NY: W. W. Norton & Company, 2012. Stiglitz, who won the Nobel Prize in economics, discusses how politics have shaped market forces and encouraged inequality. He offers a plan for a more fair and prosperous future.

Periodicals and Internet Sources

Carter, Alan and Stephen Matthews, "How tax can reduce inequality," OECD Observer. http://oecdobserver.org/news/fullstory.php/aid/3782/How_tax_can_reduce_inequality.html

Dabla-Norris, Era and Kalpana Kochhar, Nujin Suphaphiphat, Frantisek Ricka, Evridiki Tsounta, "Causes and Consequences of Income Inequality: A Global Perspective," International Monetary Fund, 2015. https://www.imf.org/external/pubs/ft/sdn/2015/sdn1513.pdf

Jain-Chandra, Sonali, "Why gender and income inequality are linked," World Economic Forum. https://www.weforum.org/agenda/2015/10/why-gender-and-income-inequality-are-linked/

Kopp, Carol, "Income Inequality Definition," Dotdash Publishing, Apr 23, 2019. https://www.investopedia.com/terms/i/income-inequality.asp

Newville, David & Emanuel Nieves, "Wealth-Building for the Wealthy Through the Tax Code Continues as Families of Color Fall Further Behind," Prosperity Now, Mar 8, 2018. https://prosperitynow.org/blog/wealth-building-wealthy-through-tax-code-continues-families-color-fall-further-behind

Powell, John A., "Six policies to reduce economic inequality," Haas Institute. https://haasinstitute.berkeley.edu/six-policies-reduce-economic-inequality

Rappaport, Mike, "Helping the Poor versus Reducing Inequality," Liberty Fund, Inc, Feb 13, 2019. https://www.lawliberty.org/2019/02/13/helping-the-poor-versus-reducing-inequality/

Shambaugh, Jay and Ryan Nunn and Stacy A. Anderson, "How racial and regional inequality affect economic opportunity," The Brookings Institution, Feb 15, 2019. https://www.brookings.edu/blog/up-front/2019/02/15/how-racial-and-regional-inequality-affect-economic-opportunity/

Surbhi S, "Difference Between Income and Wealth," Key Differences, Dec 30, 2017. https://keydifferences.com/difference-between-income-and-wealth.html

Unknown, "The Causes of Rising Income Inequality," National Bureau of Economic Research. https://www.nber.org/digest/dec08/w13982.html

Unknown, "How human rights laws are helping to address economic inequality," We Forum, Dec 21, 2018. https://www.weforum.org/agenda/2018/12/how-human-rights-laws-are-helping-to-address-economic-inequality/

Unknown, "What Is Income Inequality?" MasterClass, Jan 17, 2019. https://www.masterclass.com/articles/what-is-income-inequality#7-factors-that-lead-to-inequality

Winship, Scott, "Income Inequality Is Good For The Poor," The Federalist, Nov 5, 2014. https://thefederalist.com/2014/11/05/income-inequality-is-good-for-the-poor/

Websites

The Assistant Secretary for Planning and Evaluation (ASPE) (aspe.hhs.gov/) ASPE advises the U.S. Department of Health and Human Services on policy development. Under the website's Topics, see "Poverty Guidelines" and "Poverty Analysis."

Economic Justice Organizations (www.startguide.org/orgs/orgs04.html) Find an extensive list of organizations working against poverty and toward economic justice.

Inequality.org (inequality.org) This site tracks inequality-related news and views. It asks the question, "What can we do to narrow the staggering economic inequality that so afflicts us in almost every aspect of our lives?"

Tax Justice and Now (taxjusticenow.org) An interactive tax plan shows how different proposed plans, or your own plan, will make the tax system more or less progressive.

Index

Picture Credits

Cover KPad/Shutterstock.com; p. 10 Imagewell/Shutterstock.com; p. 14 Bettmann/Getty Images; p. 19 pathdoc/Shutterstock.com; p. 32 Blue Images/Corbis/Getty Images; p. 37 NurPhoto/Getty Images; p. 43 Bloomberg/Getty Images; p. 47 Hyejin Kang/Shutterstock.com; p. 50 Bushnell/Soifer/The Image Bank/Getty Images; p. 57 ullstein bild/Getty Images; p. 62 Andrew Olney/The Image Bank/Getty Images; p. 70 Unkas Photo/Shutterstock.com; p. 76 Toshifumi Kitamura/AFP/Getty Images; p. 79 Africa Studio/Shutterstock.com; p. 82 Dan Holm/Shutterstock.com; p. 87 Dan Kitwood/Getty Images; p. 95 Mark Van Scyoc/Shutterstock.com; p. 99 Matthew Borkoski Photography/Photolibrary/Getty Images; p. 105 Ariel Skelley/The Image Bank/Getty Images.